PALEO MONDAY TO FRIDAY

A DIET SO GOOD YOU CAN TAKE THE WEEKEND OFF!

DANIEL GREEN

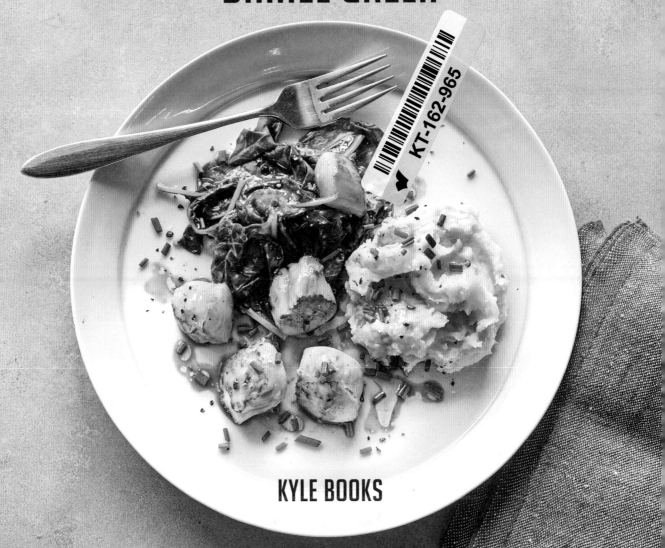

KT-162-965

KYLE BOOKS

To Georgina with love.
You are a true blessing to our lives.

First published in Great Britain in 2016 by Kyle Books
an imprint of Kyle Cathie Limited
192–198 Vauxhall Bridge Road
London SW1V 1DX
general.enquiries@kylebooks.com
www.kylebooks.com

ISBN: 978-0-85783-322-8

A CIP catalogue record for this title is available from
the British Library

Daniel Green is hereby identified as the author of this
work in accordance with Section 77 of the Copyright,
Designs and Patents Act 1988

All rights reserved. No reproduction, copy or
transmission of this publication may be made without
written permission. No paragraph of this publication
may be reproduced, copied or transmitted save
with written permission or in accordance with the
provisions of the Copyright Act 1956 (as amended).
Any person who does any unauthorised act in
relation to this publication may be liable to criminal
prosecution and civil claims for damages.

Text © Daniel Green 2016
Recipe photographs © Peter Cassidy 2016
Design © Kyle Books 2016

Editor: Vicki Murrell
Design: Anita Mangan
Recipe photography: Peter Cassidy
Food styling: Lizzie Harris
Prop styling: Iris Bromet
Production: Nic Jones

Colour reproduction by ALTA London
Printed and bound in China by C&C Offset Printing
Co., Ltd.

Important notes
All recipe analysis is per portion.

The information and advice contained in this book
are intended as a general guide to dieting and healthy
eating and are not specific to individuals or their
particular circumstances. This book is not intended
to replace treatment by a qualified practitioner.
Neither the authors nor the publishers can be held
responsible for claims arising from the inappropriate
use of any dietary regime. Do not attempt self-
diagnosis or self-treatment for serious or long-term
conditions without consulting a medical professional
or qualified practitioner.

The oven temperatures listed in this book (in celsius
and gas mark) are for fan-assisted or convection
ovens. If you have a standard oven, simply increase
the temperature by 20°C to achieve the same results.

MERTHYR TYDFIL LIBRARIES	
0458696 4	
Askews & Holts	24-Dec-2015
641.563 GRE	£14.99

CONTENTS

WHY I LOVE PALEO

In the two years since I published my last book, *The Paleo Diet*, Paleo has gone mainstream. To me, its popularity is hardly surprising as the simple principle of cutting out all the synthetic, heavily processed foods that are the cause of our 21st-century bad health and replacing them with the fresh meat, fish, nuts, seeds, fruit and vegetables that our Paleolithic ancestors thrived on gives us a food plan that is perfectly suited to our bodies. There is no weighing food, or counting calories. You eat until you are full. There is no starvation or hunger, just satisfying food that tastes great, and as a result, we're healthier and therefore happier.

And if all this sounds good, it gets even better as Paleo also operates according to an '80-20' rule, which means that if 80% of what you eat is Paleo, the remaining 20% can fall outside. I love this concept, and not because I want an excuse to eat pizza and ice cream and chocolate on my days off, but because it's what makes this diet realistic. It's what I, personally, have done for over 25 years now, since I lost 4½ stone as an overweight young adult and why over all this time, I've never put the weight back on. I've always followed the exact same rule, which is easy for us to live on and maintain. It's what we do on average that works, and it's why detox diets are so criticised. Why do we expect one detox week out of 52 to make any difference to our health or our weight? It makes sense that it's what we do most of the time that counts. So you love chocolate? Great, you can have it, just in moderation. It's when we deny ourselves things that the cravings build and build and lead to excessive, unhealthy binges and the vicious cycle of yo-yo weight loss and weight gain. It's such a relief that Paleo offers a much healthier and practical alternative!

TO ME, PALEO MONDAY TO FRIDAY IS THE PERFECT WAY OF LIFE – I HOPE YOU'LL TRY IT AND AGREE...

There are some people who don't like the 80-20 rule as they think it provides too much of an opportunity for backsliding and, of course, it's up to you. Also, if you're dealing with serious health problems or intolerances like autoimmune disease, leaky gut, arthritis and skin rashes, it makes sense to maintain a strict Paleo diet that hopefully eliminates a lot of your symptoms. However, if you are fundamentally healthy, there is no reason why you shouldn't eat a bit of dairy or a few grains or a baked potato now and again. The reality is that we're not living hunter-gatherer lifestyles! We do have times when our routines are disrupted, or we go on holiday or meet friends for dinner, and I love that Paleo acknowledges that there is sometimes more to life than food and escapes the rigid mindset that dooms almost every other diet to fail.

MONDAY TO FRIDAY

So, if you take the 80-20 Paleo rule and apply it to the week, it basically means that if you make good choices from Monday to Friday, you can relax the rules on the weekends. And so this book is all about helping you do just that. I've included recipes for breakfasts, smoothies, snacks, light meals, main meals and desserts that are simple and easy to prepare during a busy working week. Anyone can make them and the ingredients can be found anywhere. There's loads of variety, as I've picked my favourites from all over the globe and they're all so delicious and full of flavour that you'll hardly notice you're on a diet. In fact, I don't think of it as one at all. To me, Paleo Monday to Friday is the perfect way of life – I hope you'll try it and agree...

10 REASONS TO EAT THE PALEO WAY

1. It's based on unprocessed, whole foods – which means fewer additives, unhealthy trans fats and no hidden sugars or salt.

2. It's low in salt and rich in potassium – which means lower blood pressure.

3. It's high in fruit and vegetables – which means getting your 5 a day is a doddle.

4. It's low in saturated fat and high in healthy fats – which means lower cholesterol and less inflammation.

5. It's rich in protein and fibre – which means it helps you feel fuller for longer and keeps hunger pangs at bay.

6. It helps to recalibrate your metabolism – which will help you to shed any unwanted weight.

7. It's gluten-free – which helps to banish bloating and digestive problems.

8. It's low GI – which helps to avoid unhealthy spikes in blood sugar.

9. It's rich in plant-based phytochemicals – which can help reduce the risk of certain types of cancer and conditions like dementia.

10. It helps balance the pH in your body – modern diets encourage the production of acid within the body, which is believed to increase calcium loss from the bone and lead to many other health problems, including kidney stones, arthritis, fatigue, headaches, PMS and skin disorders. In contrast, the Paleo diet helps create a more alkaline environment.

YES

Pile all these good things into your supermarket trolley and you'll be guaranteed a perfect Paleo diet.

MEAT, FISH & EGGS

eggs – hen's, quail's, duck's, or even emu's

fish – don't forget fish eggs or roe, which are full of protein and essential vitamins

FRUIT & VEG

tinned fruit and veg – check the label to make sure it is sugar- and sodium-free

NUTS

nut flours – a great ingredient for baking; can be used in place of wheat flour.

nut milks – a great milk substitute. Always choose the unsweetened option, or better still, make your own.

*NB peanuts – don't forget that peanuts are not Paleo-friendly because they are legumes, not nuts.

FLAVOURINGS & SAUCES

arrowroot powder – use in place of corn-flour or wheat flour to thicken sauces

coconut aminos – a soy-free seasoning sauce made from coconut tree sap, this is a great substitute for soy sauce

curry pastes – make sure you read the label to check the ingredients. It's also very easy to make yourself.

fish sauce – if it has added fructose and sugar or hydrolysed wheat protein it is not Paleo. The Red Boat brand is only made from two ingredients (freshly caught wild black anchovies and sea salt) and is minimally processed.

meat, fish and vegetable stocks – organic and low-salt are the best options, or it's very simple to make your own

mustard – make sure it is gluten- and dairy-free

salt – sea salt is made through evaporation of ocean water or lake seawater and so undergoes little processing. Table salt is usually mined and contains additives

tomato purée – make sure it is gluten-free with no added sugar or salts

SWEETENERS

maple syrup – simply made from the sap of maple trees, this is a lovely, relatively unprocessed natural sweetener

raw honey – raw, cold-extracted honey hasn't been heat-treated or purified so contains beneficial enzymes and antioxidants.

stevia – a plant that has been used as a sweetener for centuries in Paraguay and Brazil (now commonly available as a naturally sourced sugar substitute)

COCONUT

coconut aminos – see above

coconut flour – also a great substitute for wheat flour.

coconut milk – a great substitute for milk Look for brands that don't contain guar gum or preservatives.

DRINKS

E.g. filtered or spring water, herbal tea, coconut water, freshly juiced fruit and vegetables

SEEDS

E.g. flaxseed, pumpkin seeds, sesame seeds, sunflower seeds

FRUIT & VEG

E.g. apricots, bananas, berries, cherries, citrus fruits, cranberries, dates, dragon fruit, figs, kiwis, lychees, mangos, melons, nectarines, passion fruit, peaches, pears, persimmons, plums, pomegranates, star fruit, artichokes, asparagus, aubergines, broccoli, cabbages, carrots, cauliflowers, courgettes, cucumbers, kale, kohlrabi, leeks, lettuces, marrows, okra, olives, onions, pak choi, parsnips, radishes, spinach, watercress, tomatoes, turnips, sea vegetables (kombu, nori, wakame), other seaweeds and algaes, tinned fruit and vegetables

COCONUT

E.g. coconut flour, coconut milk, shredded unsweetened coconut, coconut aminos

YES

OILS & FATS

E.g. avocado oil, coconut oil, flaxseed oil, hazelnut oil, macadamia nut oil, olive oil, sesame oil, walnut oil, lard, tallow

MEAT, FISH & EGGS

E.g. fresh meat, poultry, game and offal, fish and shellfish, eggs

SWEETENERS

E.g. raw honey, stevia, maple syrup

NUTS

E.g. almonds, Brazil nuts, cashews, chestnuts, hazelnuts, macadamias, pecans, pine nuts, pistachios, walnuts, almond flour, almond milk

FLAVOURINGS & SAUCES

E.g. fish sauce, curry paste, sea salt, truffle salt, coconut aminos, mustard, tomato purée, stocks, arrowroot powder, herbs and spices

NO

PROCESSED FOODS

WHY? Pumped full of E numbers, salt and sugar, the problem is not just with what has been added, but what has been taken away. Processed foods are often stripped of the very nutrient's dietary fibre, vitamins, minerals and phytochemicals – that are good for you.

REFINED & ADDED SUGARS

WHY? Unlike natural sugars (i.e. those you find in fruit, which come packaged with other nutrients), refined sugar provides nothing beneficial. All types of sugar (even unrefined natural sugars like honey) encourage the production of insulin which leads to the laying down of fat.

GRAINS & FOODS CONTAINING GRAINS

WHY? Grains weren't introduced into our diet until after the Agrarian Revolution, so they weren't eaten by our Paleolithic ancestors. Gluten, a protein found in grains, can irritate and damage the lining of the small intestine. This can lead to digestive problems and interfere with the absorption of nutrients from food. Furthermore, in a processed form, grains have a high GI, which means they encourage the release of insulin, which in turn triggers fat storage. They also contain phytic acid, an antinutrient that can block the absorption of important minerals.

BEANS & LEGUMES

WHY? Like cereals, beans and legumes contain antinutrients – lectins and phytic acid – which can irritate and damage the lining of the gut and cause problems such as bloating and diarrhoea. The damage caused by lectins is also thought to create a 'leaky gut', meaning that other large particles can cross the intestinal barrier and enter your blood stream. This is how food sensitivities start.

VEGETABLE & SEED OILS

WHY? These oils are high in omega-6 fatty acids (very different from heart-healthy omega-3s) and promote inflammation – one of the major causes of heart disease and other conditions such as arthritis.

POTATOES

WHY? Potatoes contain saponins – anti-nutrients that can damage the intestine. Also, they often have a high GI, which means they cause a spike in blood sugar levels that triggers the release of insulin.

DAIRY & FOODS CONTAINING DAIRY

WHY? Cow's milk is designed to help calves grow quickly, not for humans to consume throughout their lives, and many believe we lack the digestive enzymes suited to this task. In fact, humans are the only species to continue drinking milk past weaning and adults in most parts of the world do not consume many dairy products. Some estimates suggest that as much as three-quarters of the world is lactose-intolerant, to varying degrees, with symptoms including gas, bloating, cramps, indigestion, nausea, diarrhoea and constipation.

REFINED & ADDED SUGARS

E.g. sugar, fructose, high-fructose corn syrup, corn sugar, corn syrup, agave nectar, golden syrup, malt syrup, molasses, rice syrup, jam, marmalade, jelly, ketchup, hoi sin sauce, BBQ sauce

BEANS & LEGUMES

E.g. adzuki beans, baked beans, beansprouts, black beans, black-eyed peas, broad beans, cannellini beans, chickpeas, kidney beans, lentils, lima beans, mange touts, mung beans, peas, peanuts, peanut butter, pinto beans, sugar snap peas, soy and related products (tofu, miso, soya milk and soy sauce)

NO

PROCESSED FOODS

E.g. ready meals, fast food

DAIRY & FOODS CONTAINING DAIRY

E.g. milk, butter, cheese, crème fraîche, cream, ice cream, yogurt

GRAINS & FOODS CONTAINING GRAINS

E.g. flour, barley, rice, corn, sorghum, amaranth, wild rice, buckwheat, spelt, rye, quinoa, bread, pasta, cookies, biscuits, crackers, cakes, bagels, muffins, pancakes, tortilla, couscous, oats, cereal, beer

POTATOES

VEGETABLE & SEED OILS

E.g. rapeseed oil, palm oil, peanut oil, safflower oil, sunflower oil, soya bean oil, margarine

IN MODERATION

ALCOHOL

WHY? The occasional glass of wine isn't a problem and yet it is important to remember that alcohol is a toxin so 'in moderation' is key. You should also avoid alcohol that is made from foods on the 'avoid' list, such as beer (made from grain), gin (processed with grain-based alcohol), rum (made from sugar), sake (made from rice), vodka (made from potatoes) and whisky (made from grain).

CHOCOLATE

WHY? Chocolate is made from cacao which is packed with healthy chemicals like flavonoids and theobromine. However, chocolate often also contains large amounts of sugar, so ensure you choose a quality brand with a high ratio of chocolate solids (i.e. dark rather than milk).

COFFEE

WHY? Coffee can irritate the gastro-intestinal tract, decrease insulin sensitivity and hinder iron absorption. However, it is also full of antioxidants and can protect the liver, so the occasional cup will do no harm. Opt for a quality organic brand as coffee beans are often sprayed with pesticides and other toxins and don't add sugar!

SALT

WHY? A high-salt diet will increase the risk of high blood pressure and upset the acid/alkali balance within the body. I have specifically designed the recipes in this book without much salt and have used other flavours so that you won't miss it.

STARCHY VEG

WHY? The issue of starchy vegetables is one of Paleo's grey areas. Potatoes are definitely on the 'avoid' list, but other root vegetables, like sweet potatoes, don't contain the same antinutrients and don't have such an adverse effect on blood sugar levels. Many hunter-gatherer groups, such as the Kitavans of Papua New Guinea, regularly eat yams, sweet potatoes, taro, and cassava (tapioca), and don't suffer any adverse effects. For this reason I include them here in the 'in moderation' group.

SWEETENERS

WHY? The body processes all forms of sugar in the same way (even honey produces an insulin response in the body), so I recommend you only use raw honey, maple syrup or stevia (in moderation) as sweeteners. Raw honey is honey in its purest, most unprocessed form (it still contains many of the nutrients that the bees put into it). Stevia is a natural, plant-sourced, calorie-free sugar substitute.

VINEGAR

WHY? Strictly speaking, vinegar wasn't introduced to the human diet until after the Agrarian Revolution, so it wasn't around in the Paleolithic times – if you do want to use vinegar in moderation, choose apple cider vinegar, balsamic or red/white wine vinegar rather than barley malt vinegar. Vinegar can upset the acid/alkali balance within the body, so use it only in moderation.

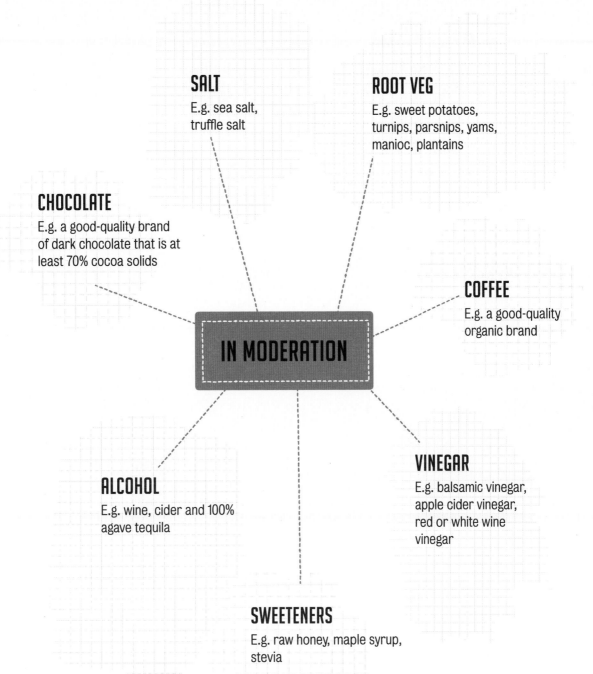

SALT
E.g. sea salt, truffle salt

ROOT VEG
E.g. sweet potatoes, turnips, parsnips, yams, manioc, plantains

CHOCOLATE
E.g. a good-quality brand of dark chocolate that is at least 70% cocoa solids

COFFEE
E.g. a good-quality organic brand

IN MODERATION

ALCOHOL
E.g. wine, cider and 100% agave tequila

VINEGAR
E.g. balsamic vinegar, apple cider vinegar, red or white wine vinegar

SWEETENERS
E.g. raw honey, maple syrup, stevia

BREAKFASTS
& BRUNCHES

SUN-DRIED TOMATO OMELETTE
WITH MEXICAN SALSA

When I spent time in Mexico, I discovered how salsas are such a great accompaniment to eggs. They're so fresh and spicy and make a fantastic breakfast or brunch, especially in the summer.

340 CALORIES | 23G FAT | 4.5G SATURATES | 11.5G CARBS | 11G SUGAR | 1.1G SALT | 21G PROTEIN | 3.5G FIBRE

SERVES 2

4 eggs

2 egg whites

sea salt and freshly ground black pepper

olive oil spray, for frying

40g sun-dried tomatoes in olive oil, drained and finely sliced

2 spring onions, sliced

for the salsa

4 plum tomatoes, deseeded and finely chopped

6 fresh basil leaves, finely chopped

a handful of fresh coriander leaves, finely chopped

¼ white onion, finely chopped

juice of ½ lime

1 small Jalapeno pepper, finely chopped

1. First make the salsa: Place all the ingredients in a large bowl and mix together well.

2. Break the eggs into a separate bowl, lightly season and beat together with a fork.

3. Place a frying pan over a high heat, spray with a little olive oil and add the eggs, tilting the pan to spread the mix evenly over the base, then lower the heat to medium. After a minute or two, use a spatula to pull the outer edges of the omelette into the centre. The liquid, uncooked egg will fill the space and ensure the omelette cooks evenly and the base doesn't burn.

4. When almost all the egg is cooked, add the sun-dried tomato, then use a spatula again to flip one side of the omelette over so it is folded in half.

5. Take off the heat, rest for 30 seconds and then serve immediately with the spring onion scattered over and the salsa on the side.

TIP You can make this the night before as it keeps well in the refrigerator. Take the chilli seeds out if you don't want too much of a kick too early in the morning!

KALE & EGGS
WITH GRILLED TOMATOES

Kale is very close to spinach in nutritional values (loaded with vitamins, minerals, antioxidants and phytonutrients) but it has a little more texture and strength so it holds its shape when you cook with it. Also, its bulk means it's filling and sets you up for the day, which makes it perfect for breakfast.

467 CALORIES | 34.5G FAT | 7G SATURATES | 7G CARBS | 7G SUGAR | 0.8G SALT | 28.5G PROTEIN | 6.5G FIBRE

SERVES 2

1 tablespoon pine nuts

2 tablespoons olive oil

4 large tomatoes, thickly sliced

200g kale leaves, destemmed

6–8 fresh basil leaves, shredded

6 eggs

1. Place a large non-stick frying pan over a medium-high heat and, when hot, toast the pine nuts (with no oil) until they turn brown – this will only take a minute or two. Transfer the pine nuts to a dish and set aside.

2. Add a drizzle of oil to the same pan and fry the tomatoes for about 2 minutes on each side. Again, transfer to a dish and set aside.

3. Now turn up the heat, add a tablespoon of oil to the pan and stir-fry the kale for a few minutes until it chars and turns a little crispy. Add the shredded basil and toasted pine nuts to the pan and toss together.

4. Meanwhile, heat the remaining oil in a large frying pan and, when hot, crack in each egg, being careful not to crowd the pan. Cover and leave for a few minutes, then check the white is cooked, lift out and transfer to a plate.

5. Serve the eggs immediately with the fried tomato and kale and garnish with a little fresh basil.

TIP This recipe serves up 3 eggs per person. It may seem like a lot but scientific research has debunked the myth that dietary cholesterol causes heart disease and actually proves that eating up to 3 whole eggs per day are a great way for a healthy person to stay healthy. Enjoy!

½ EGG & ½ EGG WHITE OMELETTE

Eggs are high in dietary cholesterol (185mg) and this is all contained in the egg's yolk, so back when scientists thought that dietary cholesterol was linked to blood cholesterol and heart disease, egg yolks started to get a bad name. This is a shame as the yolk is in fact a powerhouse of nutrition and the fat it contains even helps to reduce LDL (bad cholesterol) in the blood. However, as many of the breakfast recipes in this book contain many eggs, I've made an omelette here with a 2:1 ratio of egg white to egg yolk as, for me, it still has the perfect golden colour and creamy texture but tastes a little less rich.

155 CALORIES | 10G FAT | 2.5G SATURATES | 0G CARBS | 0G SUGAR | 0.6G SALT | 17G PROTEIN | 0G FIBRE

SERVES 2

3 eggs

3 egg whites

sea salt and freshly ground
black pepper

1 teaspoon olive oil

your choice of fillings
(see below)

1. Break the eggs into a bowl, lightly season and beat together with a fork.

2. Place a frying pan over a high heat and add the olive oil, then fry the filling ingredients of your choice (see below) for a minute or two until cooked.

3. Add the eggs, tilting the pan to spread the mix evenly over the base, then lower the heat to medium. After a minute or two, use a spatula to pull the outer edges of the omelette into the centre. The uncooked egg will fill the space and ensure the omelette cooks evenly and the base doesn't burn.

4. When almost all the egg is cooked, use a spatula again to flip one side of the omelette over so it is folded in half. Take off the heat, rest for 30 seconds and then serve immediately.

TIP All these ingredients taste delicious finely chopped in an omelette. I recommend using whatever meat and vegetables you have in your refrigerator at the time as a way of keeping the flavours and combinations nice and varied: sun-dried tomatoes, onions, mushrooms, peppers, tomatoes, ham, chicken, turkey, lean bacon, chives, flat-leaf parsley.

RED ONION & SPINACH OMELETTE

Eggs are among the most nutritious foods on the planet and spinach is a superfood loaded with health benefits (full of iron, vitamins and minerals) so this omelette makes a breakfast of champions.

181 CALORIES | 10G FAT | 2.5G SATURATES | 2G CARBS | 1.5G SUGAR | 0.7G SALT | 20G PROTEIN | 1.1G FIBRE

SERVES 2

1 teaspoon olive oil

¼ red onion, finely chopped

100g fresh spinach

3 whole eggs

4 egg whites

sea salt and freshly ground
    black pepper

1. Place the olive oil in a non-stick frying pan over a high heat. Add the onion and fry for a minute, then add the spinach and cook until wilted. Transfer to a plate and set aside.

2. Crack the eggs into a bowl, season lightly and beat with a fork.

3. Now make one omelette at a time: Tip half the egg mix into the hot pan, tilting to spread the mix evenly over the base, then scatter half the cooked onion and spinach over the top.

4. After a minute or two, use a spatula to pull the outer edges of the omelette into the centre. The uncooked egg will fill the space and ensure the omelette cooks evenly and the base doesn't burn.

5. When almost all the egg is cooked, use a spatula again to flip one side of the omelette over so it is folded in half.

6. Take off the heat, rest for 30 seconds and then serve immediately. Repeat steps 3–5 for the second omelette.

TIP The omelette will continue to cook after you have taken it off the heat so don't overcook it in the pan and don't rest it for too long either. Serve while it is still nice and hot.

PORK PATTIES
WITH HOMEMADE TOMATO KETCHUP

This dish is a great alternative to a traditional meaty cooked breakfast and also makes a great lunch or dinner, served with a nice fresh salad.

274 CALORIES | 10G FAT | 4G SATURATES | 12G CARBS | 10G SUGAR | 0.3G SALT | 33G PROTEIN | 1.5G FIBRE

SERVES 4

olive oil spray, for frying

a handful of flat-leaf parsley,
   to garnish

for the tomato ketchup

1 x 400g tin tomato sauce

85g tomato purée

60ml white vinegar

1½ tablespoons maple syrup

for the patties

450g lean pork mince

1 egg

1 teaspoon ground cumin

1 teaspoon dried crushed
   chillies

1 tablespoon chopped
   fresh parsley

1 small white onion,
   finely chopped

1 garlic clove, crushed

2 tablespoons homemade
   tomato ketchup
   (see above)

1. First make the tomato ketchup: Place all the ingredients in a saucepan and stir to combine. Bring to the boil over a medium heat, then turn down to a simmer, cover, turn off the heat and let stand for 5 minutes.

2. Meanwhile, make the patties: Place all the ingredients in a large bowl and use your hands to mix together well. When thoroughly combined, shape the mince into 5cm-wide patties. You should have enough to make a dozen or so.

3. Place a large frying pan over a high heat and lightly spray with oil. When hot, fry the patties for 2–3 minutes on each side until cooked through.

4. Stir the tomato ketchup again and serve with the patties with a little fresh parsley to garnish.

TIP You can buy your own pork and mince it yourself in a food processor. In fact, I recommend doing this whenever you cook with mince as then you know exactly how fresh it is and what's in it.

BACON & EGGS

The Great British Fry-up started to get a bad name when fat was demonised back in the 1950s. However, there really is no evidence that high-fat foods lead to heart disease and weight gain. In fact, they fill you up faster (so you'll eat less) and for longer than high-carb foods so forget the toast and the hash browns and you can enjoy this guiltless pleasure.

480 CALORIES | 36G FAT | 11G SATURATES | 3G CARBS | 3G SUGAR | 2.7G SALT | 35G PROTEIN | 1.5G FIBRE

SERVES 4

1½ tablespoons olive oil

12 small mushrooms, cleaned and quartered

3 plum tomatoes, halved

12 lean rashers back bacon, trimmed of fat

12 eggs (3 per person)

fresh cracked black pepper

4 sprigs of fresh parsley

1. Heat 1 tablespoon olive oil in a large non-stick frying pan and stir-fry the mushrooms for 2–3 minutes over a high heat. Lower the heat a little, add the tomatoes and cook for another 2–3 minutes, turning them halfway through, then transfer to a plate and keep warm.

2. Place the bacon in the same pan and fry over a medium heat for a minute or two on each side.

3. Meanwhile, spray another large non-stick frying pan with a little oil and, when hot, crack in each egg, being careful not to crowd the pan. Cover and leave for a few minutes, then check the white is cooked, lift out and transfer to a plate.

4. Serve everything together with a sprinkle of cracked pepper and fresh parsley for colour.

TIP The best way to clean mushrooms is to wipe them with kitchen paper. This doesn't add any moisture and yet still cleans them well.

MUSHROOM & ONION WRAP

The coconut flour gives this pancake a lovely sweet flavour. It can be quite delicate so allow it to sit in the pan and firm up a little before you flip it.

416 CALORIES | 32G FAT | 3G SATURATES | 12.5G CARBS | 5G SUGAR | 0.2G SALT | 15G PROTEIN | 6G FIBRE

SERVES 4

olive oil spray, for frying

100g button mushrooms, roughly chopped

¼ red onion, finely sliced

3 egg whites

4 tablespoons coconut flour

1. Place a large non-stick frying pan over a high heat, spray with a little olive oil and stir-fry the mushrooms for 3 minutes or so until they start to brown. Add the onion and stir-fry for an additional 2–3 minutes, then remove from the pan and keep warm.

2. Crack the egg into a small bowl, add the egg white and beat lightly with a fork. Add the coconut flour and stir to combine.

3. Place the clean non-stick pan back on a medium heat and spray with a little olive oil. Ladle a quarter of the pancake batter into the pan and swirl to coat the base evenly. Leave to cook for 2 minutes or so. When firm, flip the pancake and cook the other side for 2 minutes. When lightly brown, add a quarter of the onion and mushroom mix and then fold the pancake over so the filling is sealed inside.

4. Make the remaining pancakes, then simply slide onto a plate and serve immediately.

TIP Coconut flour is a great Paleo-friendly alternative to wheat flour – it's nutrient-rich, full of fibre and also low-GI, which means it supports a healthy metabolism and stable blood sugar levels.

POACHED EGGS
ON SMOKED SALMON & SPINACH

Poaching is probably the very best way to cook eggs – it's so easy and you don't add a single drop of extra fat. However, don't forget to use the freshest eggs you can afford as it'll make all the difference.

617 CALORIES | 38G FAT | 10G SATURATES | 2G CARBS | 2G SUGAR | 7G SALT | 66G PROTEIN | 3G FIBRE

SERVES 2

a dash of white vinegar

6 eggs

200g spinach leaves

350g Scottish smoked salmon, thinly sliced

a twist of black pepper

1. Bring a large saucepan of water to the boil and add a dash of white vinegar. Crack each egg individually into a ramekin or small cup and then slide it into the water. It's important not to overcrowd the pan so I recommend you only cook three at a time. Cook the eggs for a minute at a rolling boil, then reduce to a simmer and cook for a further 2 minutes.

2. Remove the eggs with a slotted spoon and place briefly in a pan of cold water to remove any trace of vinegar, then place on a sheet of kitchen paper.

3. Place a pile of spinach leaves on each individual plate and top with smoked salmon and three poached eggs. Finish with a twist of black pepper and serve immediately.

TIP Free-range chickens grubbing in a field are far healthier than ones kept in cages and studies have shown their eggs are nutritionally superior.

JAPANESE EGG CUSTARDS

These little steamed egg custards are traditionally served for breakfast in Japan. They're delicious and savoury and keep you feeling full right up until lunch. I also like to serve these with finely sliced mushrooms or spring onions and you can substitute the salmon for small prawns if you like.

168 CALORIES | 10G FAT | 2G SATURATES | 1.5G CARBS | 1G SUGAR | 0.8G SALT | 18G PROTEIN | 2G FIBRE

SERVES 4

4 eggs

2 egg whites

vegetable stock or dashi (you need equal ratio of stock to egg)

120g flaked cooked salmon

4 large broccoli florets, quartered

1. Crack the eggs into a medium-sized bowl and, using chopsticks, lightly whisk until blended, without incorporating too much air. Stir in the dashi or stock (a 50:50 ratio of egg to stock).

2. Divide the flaked salmon between four small serving bowls or ramekins and pour the egg mixture on top. Cover the bowls or wrap them in clingfilm and steam over a low heat (the water should be at a gentle simmer) for 15–20 minutes, or until the eggs are set – a bamboo steamer is great for this.

3. Immediately transfer the bowls to the refrigerator to chill for at least 3 hours or overnight.

4. Unwrap the custards. Place the broccoli florets in a bamboo steamer over a pan of gently simmering water and steam for 3–4 minutes.

5. Top the custards with the broccoli and serve.

TIP In order to achieve the perfect velvety smooth texture, cook these little custards on the lowest heat you can manage.

COOKED APPLES IN MAPLE SYRUP
WITH AN ALMOND CRUMB

This is the perfect warming, filling breakfast to eat on a cold winter's morning.
Or it could make a very tasty pudding too.

544 CALORIES | 29G FAT | 2.5G SATURATES | 52G CARBS | 49G SUGAR | 0G SALT | 13G PROTEIN | 5G FIBRE

SERVES 2

4 apples, peeled, cored and
  roughly chopped

100ml water

1 teaspoon ground cinnamon

2 tablespoons maple syrup

100g almond flour

a handful of fresh blackberries

1. Preheat the grill to its highest setting.

2. Place the apples in a saucepan with 100ml
   water, then add the cinnamon and 1 tablespoon
   of maple syrup. Bring to the boil, cover and
   simmer for about 7 minutes, then remove the
   lid and cook for a further minute to allow any
   excess liquid to evaporate.

3. Divide the cooked apple between four
   ovenproof serving bowls and cover each one
   with almond flour and a drizzle of maple syrup.
   Place under the grill for a minute or so, being
   careful not to burn.

4. Serve with a few fresh blackberries on the side.

TIP Almond flour has a wonderful texture and flavour,
plus it's very low in carbs, full of manganese and
vitamin E and monounsaturated fats, and contains a
very healthy amount of protein.

BERRY COMPOTE
WITH A COCONUT CRUST

This breakfast is excellent at filling the gap when you are craving carbs.
I recommend that you make it the night before, then simply place it
under the grill in the morning.

231 CALORIES | 6G FAT | 4G SATURATES | 28G CARBS | 14G SUGAR | 0.2G SALT | 8G PROTEIN | 15G FIBRE

SERVES 4

350g blackberries

170g raspberries

30ml water

2 tablespoons maple syrup

110g coconut flour

1 egg, beaten

50ml unsweetened almond
  milk

1. Preheat the grill to its highest setting.

2. Place the blackberries and raspberries in a
   saucepan with 30ml water and add the maple
   syrup. Bring to the boil and cook for 2–3
   minutes, then turn down the heat and simmer
   for 4–5 minutes (so the berries keep their shape).

3. Meanwhile, mix the coconut flour with the egg
   and almond milk and break the mixture up so it
   resembles a crumble.

4. Divide the cooked berries, reserving the juices,
   between four ovenproof serving bowls and
   top with the crumble mix. Drizzle over a little
   more maple syrup and place under a hot grill
   for 3–4 minutes or so, being careful not to
   burn. Serve warm with a drizzle of the reserved
   berry juice.

TIP Fresh fruit is great and 'fresh is best' is often used as a
healthy eating mantra. However, research has shown
that frozen fruit and veg actually provide the same health
benefits as fresh and can even retain their nutritional value
for longer as they're preserved at their peak. Frozen
berries work perfectly for this recipe as they are cooked
down and therefore don't have to look freshly picked
and beautiful.

SMOOTHIES

MANGO SMOOTHIE

This makes such a delicious, sweet and creamy smoothie, and it's perfectly refreshing.

138 CALORIES | 1.5G FAT | 0.5G SATURATES | 26G CARBS | 26G SUGAR | 0.2G SALT | 2G PROTEIN | 5G FIBRE

SERVES 2

1 medium mango, peeled and destoned

240ml unsweetened almond milk

juice of 1 orange

juice of ½ lemon

1. Place all the ingredients in a blender and whiz until smooth.

2. Pour into a glass and serve immediately.

STRAWBERRY ENERGISER

I know that coffee is not strictly Paleo but I also know that most people need the odd caffeine fix now and again. The best advice I think is to save it for those times when you need it most...

64 CALORIES | 2G FAT | 0.2G SATURATES | 9G CARBS | 9G SUGAR | 0.1G SALT | 1G PROTEIN | 4G FIBRE

SERVES 2

200g fresh strawberries, destemmed

1 shot espresso coffee

240ml unsweetened almond milk

8–10 ice cubes

1. Place all the ingredients in a blender and whiz until smooth.

2. Pour into a glass and serve immediately.

MORNING ENERGISER

The banana here will provide you with plenty of energy. However, you can also add a little coffee (see Tip below) if it's a day off.

104 CALORIES | 1.5G FAT | 0.2G SATURATES | 20G CARBS | 19G SUGAR | 0.2G SALT | 1.5G PROTEIN | 0.7G FIBRE

SERVES 2

300ml unsweetened almond milk

1 tablespoon maple syrup

1 ripe banana

1. Place all the ingredients in a blender and whiz until smooth.

2. Pour into glasses and serve immediately.

TIP Coffee is a no on strict Paleo, but if it's the weekend and you feel you need a little extra energy, add 1 freshly made espresso shot to the blender before you whiz.

KALE & BERRY SMOOTHIE

This is a great detox drink. Kale is the no. 1 superfood of the moment, and with good reason – it's incredibly low in calories and yet amazingly rich in nutrients (especially the minerals many of us are deficient in) and if you simply eat more kale you will significantly improve the total nutrient content in your diet.

123 CALORIES | TRACE FAT | TRACE SATURATES | 22G CARBS | 22G SUGAR | 0G SALT | 3G PROTEIN | 7G FIBRE

SERVES 2

50g kale leaves, destemmed

350ml freshly squeezed orange juice

200g strawberries, hulled

100g raspberries

1. Place all the ingredients in a blender and whiz until smooth.

2. Pour into glasses and serve immediately.

TIP Smoothies taste best when they are freshest. The ingredients can separate and the texture can become thick or gelatinous if they're left to sit and so I always recommend you drink them straight away.

ASIAN FRUIT SMOOTHIE WITH PASSION FRUIT

Most fruits from Southeast Asia are deliciously sweet and mango and papaya are no exception. However, as they are so high in sugar (and therefore also high in carbs), use a little sparingly and save for a treat.

132 CALORIES | 3.5G FAT | 2G SATURATES | 20G CARBS | 20G SUGAR | 0.1G SALT | 2G PROTEIN | 5.5G FIBRE

SERVES 2

½ small mango, peeled and de-stoned

½ small papaya, peeled and deseeded

175ml unsweetened almond milk

60ml light coconut milk

2 passion fruit, halved

1. Place the mango and papaya in a blender with the milks and whiz until smooth.

2. Pour into glasses, then scoop out the seeds of the passion fruit and float in the top of each smoothie. Serve immediately.

FROZEN BERRY SMOOTHIE

Frozen berries are very nutritious as the berries are picked and frozen when they're ripe and in their prime. However try not to keep them in the freezer for longer than 6 months to a year.

80 CALORIES | 0G FAT | 0G SATURATES | 16G CARBS | 16G SUGAR | 0G SALT | 2G PROTEIN | 3G FIBRE

SERVES 2

250g frozen berries (a mix of raspberries, blackberries and strawberries are best)

240ml freshly squeezed orange juice

3–4 sprigs fresh mint (optional)

1. Place the berries with the orange juice in a blender and whiz until smooth. Add a little more juice to thin out the mixture if it becomes a little thick.

2. Pour into glasses and serve with a sprig of mint.

CUCUMBER & MINT DETOX

This is the BEST smoothie ever – fresh, filling and incredibly tasty. If I were you,
I'd try this before any of the others.

123 CALORIES | 8G FAT | 1.5G SATURATES | 8G CARBS | 8G SUGAR | 0G SALT | 3G PROTEIN | 3G FIBRE

SERVES 2

¾ cucumber, sliced

2 tablespoons torn fresh mint leaves

juice of 2 oranges (add the flesh if
you want a thicker smoothie)

½ ripe avocado, peeled and
destoned

4–6 ice cubes

1. Place the cucumber, mint and orange
juice in a blender and whiz until smooth.
Add the avocado and whiz again, adding
a little more juice if the mixture becomes
a little thick and your blender struggles.

2. Pour into glasses over ice and serve with
a garnish of fresh mint.

TIP Cucumbers are great for detox as they're diuretics
and so help you to avoid water retention and flush
toxins out of the body.

WATERMELON & MINT SMOOTHIE

I love this drink as it tastes of summer, even during the darkest winter.
Simply increase or decrease the quantity of mint to suit your taste.

54 CALORIES | 0G FAT | 0G SATURATES | 11G CARBS | 11G SUGAR | 0G SALT | 0.8G PROTEIN | 0.2G FIBRE

SERVES 2

340g watermelon flesh,
cut into chunks

2–3 tablespoons fresh mint leaves

8–10 ice cubes

1. Place the ingredients in a blender and
whiz until smooth.

2. Pour into glasses over ice and serve
immediately.

TIP On a weekend, I recommend you serve this over ice
and add a shot of Cîroc vodka, which is made from
grapes rather than potatoes!

VITAMIN C BLAST

This refreshing drink provides you with more nutrients than any vitamin C pill, plus it will also boost your immune system, ward off colds and infections and taste delicious.

154 CALORIES | 0G FAT | 0G SATURATES | 30G CARBS | 30G SUGAR | 0G SALT | 3G PROTEIN | 6G FIBRE

SERVES 2

3 oranges, peeled and excess pith removed

2 grapefruits, peeled and excess pith removed

juice of 1 lemon

1 tablespoon torn fresh mint leaves

1. Place the orange and grapefruit segments in a blender with the lemon juice and torn mint and whiz until smooth.

2. Pour into glasses and serve immediately.

COCONUT MILK & MANGO SMOOTHIE

This smoothie provides a great natural energy boost, plus it's very filling and you won't need anything else for breakfast.

263 CALORIES | 16G FAT | 13G SATURATES | 26G CARBS | 24G SUGAR | 0.1G SALT | 2.5G PROTEIN | 5G FIBRE

SERVES 2

175ml coconut milk

90ml unsweetened almond milk

1 small ripe mango, peeled and destoned

½ banana, peeled

1. Place all the ingredients in a blender and whiz until smooth.

2. Pour into glasses and serve immediately.

ALMOND BERRY BLAST

I recommend you source the unsweetened version of almond milk if you are watching your weight as the 'original' varieties often contain as much as 7 grams of sugar per carton.

117 CALORIES | 2G FAT | 0.2G SATURATES | 18G CARBS | 18G SUGAR | 0.2G SALT | 2.6G PROTEIN | 7G FIBRE

SERVES 2

300ml unsweetened almond milk

150g strawberries

100g raspberries

100g blackberries

½ ripe banana

1. Place all the ingredients in a blender and whiz until smooth.

2. Pour into glasses and serve immediately.

LIGHT MEALS, SNACKS & SIDES

EGG & COURGETTE MUFFINS

These make a great protein-packed snack or breakfast. If you want a fluffier, soufflé-type version, whisk the egg whites until they form soft peaks, then add the remaining ingredients.

158 CALORIES | 9G FAT | 2.5G SATURATES | 2.5G CARBS | 2G SUGAR | 0.5G SALT | 15G PROTEIN | 1.5G FIBRE

SERVES 4

150g salad leaves, to serve

for the muffins
olive oil spray
6 eggs
3 egg whites
1 large courgette, coarsely grated
½ red onion, finely chopped
a handful of fresh basil leaves,
    finely chopped
1 teaspoon crushed black pepper

1. Preheat the oven to 180°C/gas mark 4 and lightly grease a muffin tin with cooking spray.

2. In a large bowl, beat the eggs well, then add the remaining muffin ingredients and stir to combine.

3. Pour or spoon the mixture into four muffin cups, almost all the way full, then bake until cooked through or lightly golden, about 18–20 minutes.

4. Serve with a fresh green salad.

EGG & TUNA MUFFINS

190 CALORIES | 9G FAT | 2.5G SATURATES | 2G CARBS | 2G SUGAR | 0.6G SALT | 22G PROTEIN | 1.2G FIBRE

SERVES 4

150g salad leaves, to serve

for the muffins
olive oil spray
8 button mushrooms, finely chopped
6 eggs
3 egg whites
½ red onion, finely chopped
1 x 140g tin tuna in water, drained
a handful of fresh basil leaves,
    finely chopped
1 teaspoon crushed black pepper

1. Preheat the oven to 180°C/gas mark 4 and lightly grease a muffin tin with cooking spray.

2. Place a non-stick frying pan over a medium-high heat, spray with a little oil and sauté the mushrooms for 2–3 minutes until golden brown, then set aside to cool.

3. In a large bowl, beat the eggs well, then add the remaining muffin ingredients and stir to combine.

4. Pour or spoon the mixture into four muffin cups, almost all the way full, then bake until cooked through or lightly golden, about 18–20 minutes. Serve with a fresh green salad.

TRUFFLE OIL AVOCADO

This is so simple and yet so tasty, I could eat copious amounts of it all day long (it goes perfectly with either grilled steak or chicken). It also feels like a real indulgence so it's great when you need a treat but don't want to fall off the wagon too hard or too fast.

497 CALORIES | 51G FAT | 9G SATURATES | 3G CARBS | 0.7G SUGAR | 0G SALT | 3G PROTEIN | 7G FIBRE

1 avocado, peeled and destoned
2 tablespoons white truffle oil
juice of ½ large lemon

1. Place all the ingredients in a food processor (or alternatively use a hand-held electric blender) and whiz until almost smooth.

2. Serve with crudités or grilled steak or chicken.

AVOCADO MAYO

Commercial mayonnaise is often full of preservatives and offers you very little in terms of nutrition. However, this homemade version using mild-flavoured avocado oil is the opposite. It tastes just like traditional mayo but is incredibly healthy and delicious.

918 CALORIES | 99G FAT | 16G SATURATES | 0.5G CARBS | 0.5G SUGAR | 0G SALT | 6G PROTEIN | 0G FIBRE

2 egg yolks
juice of ½ lemon
120ml avocado oil
pinch of sea salt and freshly ground black pepper

1. Place the egg yolks and lemon juice in a food processor and whiz to combine, then begin to pour in the avocado oil very slowly, tablespoon by tablespoon.

2. As the avocado oil gradually mixes in, it will begin to thicken and create a mayo-like consistency. Add more oil as needed to help thicken it even more, then season to taste.

3. Season with salt and pepper and place the mayo in a container and refrigerate.

AVOCADO TOMATILLO SAUCE

This sauce can be served as a dip with crudités or used to spice up any simple fillet of fish, chicken or beef.

850 CALORIES | 62G FAT | 13G SATURATES | 42G CARBS | 37G SUGAR | 2G SALT | 14G PROTEIN | 33G FIBRE

4 fresh tomatillos, peeled

2 avocados, peeled and destoned

3 garlic cloves

juice of 1–1½ limes

6–10 sprigs of fresh coriander

¼–½ teaspoon sea salt

for the crudités

300g carrots, peeled and cut into sticks

300g celery, cut into sticks

½ cucumber, cut into sticks

a bunch of radish, topped and tailed and quartered

1. Bring a pan of lightly salted water to the boil and cook the tomatillos for about 3–4 minutes to soften. Allow to cool.

2. Place all the ingredients in a food processor and whiz until smooth. Serve straight away with crudités.

TIP Tomatillos are also called *tomate verde* in Mexico (which means green tomato) and are a staple in Mexican cooking (their delicious green salsas). They're best when they're about the size of a cherry tomato and have a wonderful citrusy sweet flavour. To prepare, simply destem, remove the papery outer layer and wash.

ROASTED VEGETABLES
WITH WHITE TRUFFLE SALT

I think this is one of the easiest, simplest and best ways to eat vegetables as the roasting brings out their sweet flavour and makes them deliciously tender.

295 CALORIES | 14G FAT | 2G SATURATES | 22G CARBS | 20G SUGAR | 2.7G SALT | 10G PROTEIN | 17G FIBRE

SERVES 2-4

400g carrots, topped, tailed and halved lengthways

12 button mushrooms, stems removed

2 leeks, trimmed and sliced

a handful of asparagus, trimmed

1 fennel, cut into wedges

2 courgettes, topped, tailed, halved lengthways and cut into large chunks

1 tablespoon chopped fresh thyme

2 tablespoons olive oil

1 tablespoon balsamic vinegar

1 teaspoon white truffle salt

1. Preheat the oven to 200°C/gas mark 6.

2. In a large bowl, mix the vegetables together with the thyme, olive oil and vinegar.

3. Tip all the vegetables into a large roasting tin and roast for 10 minutes, then take out of the oven, give the tin a shake and roast for a further 10 minutes or until soft, golden and cooked through.

4. Sprinkle over white truffle salt and serve immediately.

TIP Truffle salt is sea salt infused with the Italian delicacy of dried truffles, which lends it a deliciously rich, earthy flavour. It makes a great alternative seasoning (try it with eggs) and is a great thing to have on hand in your Paleo store cupboard.

SALMON FISHCAKES
WITH ASIAN DRESSING

This is one of the recipes that I come back to time and time again. I included it in my very first cookbook, back in 2002, but every time I make the recipe, I refine it a little and this version contains even more flavour.

545 CALORIES | 43G FAT | 7.5G SATURATES | 3G CARBS | 2.5G SUGAR | 0.3G SALT | 35G PROTEIN | 2.5G FIBRE

SERVES 4

1 tablespoon olive oil,
  for frying

150g mixed salad leaves, to
  serve

for the Asian dressing

2.5cm cube fresh ginger,
  grated

60ml sesame oil

1 tablespoon sesame seeds

juice of ½ lemon

1 garlic clove, crushed

for the fishcakes

4 x skinless salmon fillets,
  roughly chopped

1 teaspoon sesame oil

1 tablespoon sesame seeds

1 egg

1 egg white

2.5cm cube fresh ginger, grated

1 bird's eye chilli, finely sliced

4 spring onions, finely sliced

½ red onion, finely sliced

a handful of fresh coriander,
  finely chopped

1. First make the Asian dressing: Simply place all the ingredients in a bowl and whisk well to combine.

2. Now make the fishcakes: Place the salmon, sesame oil, sesame seeds, egg, ginger, chilli, spring onions, red onion and coriander in a food processor and blitz together, making sure you retain a little texture.

3. On a clean surface, divide the fishcake mixture and carefully shape into little patties about 2.5cm thick. Transfer to a plate, cover and chill for 30 minutes (or up to a day).

4. Heat the olive oil in a large, non-stick sauté pan over a high heat and cook about 4–5 fish cakes at a time (don't overcrowd the pan or they won't brown up as they should). Cook for a minute, then lower the heat a little, turn and cook for another 60–90 seconds (they are small so will cook quickly).

5. Repeat until all the fishcakes are cooked and serve warm, drizzled with a little Asian dressing, and a mixed leaf salad.

CRAB & SALMON TOWER

This is a great dinner party dish as it's so simple but never fails to impress and no one will ever guess you are on a diet.

452 CALORIES | 30G FAT | 5.5G SATURATES | 3G CARBS | 2G SUGAR | 1.4G SALT | 41G PROTEIN | 3.5G FIBRE

SERVES 4

2 x 180g tins crab meat, drained

½ red onion, finely chopped

1 tablespoon olive oil

a handful of fresh dill, roughly chopped

juice of 1 lemon

sea salt and freshly ground black pepper

1 tablespoon sesame seeds

450g fresh salmon, cubed (or smoked salmon, finely chopped)

1 avocado, peeled and destoned

a squeeze of lemon

2 spring onions, finely chopped

150g green salad leaves

a drizzle of olive oil

1. Place the crab meat in a bowl with the onion, olive oil, dill and lemon juice. Mix well, season to taste and set aside.

2. In another bowl, scatter the sesame seeds over the salmon and mix until thoroughly coated.

3. In another bowl, mash the avocado with a squeeze of lemon. Season to taste, add the spring onion and mash into the avocado.

4. Place a pastry ring in the centre of each plate and spoon in a quarter of the crab mix, pushing it down well into the mould. Add a layer of avocado and finish with the salmon, pressing everything down so the tower will hold its shape when you remove the pastry ring. Repeat this for each serving.

5. Serve with a fresh green salad, a drizzle of olive oil and a pinch of salt.

TIP If you want to splash out, substitute fresh crab meat for tinned.

SUSHI

Over the following pages, I've included lots and lots of sushi recipes as they are filling and flavourful and full of everything we love about Japanese cuisine, but leaving out the rice makes them almost carb-free too – perfect for a snack or a lunch on the run.

AVOCADO & SPICY TUNA

314 CALORIES | 18G FAT | 3.5G SATURATES | 3.5G CARBS | 3G SUGAR | 0.2G SALT | 31.5G PROTEIN | 4G FIBRE

SERVES 2

½ avocado, chopped into small cubes

225g fresh tuna, chopped into small cubes

¼ red onion, finely chopped

1 tablespoon sesame seeds

1 tablespoon sesame oil

¼ red chilli, finely chopped (deseeded too, if you like)

a handful of fresh coriander, finely chopped

2 nori (seaweed) sheets

1 spring onion, trimmed and sliced lengthways

¼ cucumber, peeled and sliced lengthways into quarters

1. Place the avocado, tuna, red onion, sesame seeds, sesame oil, chilli and coriander in a bowl and mix together.

2. Lay a nori sheet, shiny side down, on the mat and spread half of the tuna mix across the sheet in a thin layer, but leaving the furthest edge clear.

3. Lay the spring onion and cucumber down the middle of each sheet, then use the mat to roll the sushi up, applying gentle pressure to keep the roll tight.

4. When you get to the far edge of the nori, dab it with a little water to seal it up. Trim the ends with a sharp knife, then slice the long roll into half, and then half again. Repeat with the second nori sheet, then serve.

TIP A bamboo mat or makisu can be very useful as it helps maintain even pressure from all sides when rolling it up.

TURKEY & ASPARAGUS

Turkey is so full of protein that one serving (110g) provides 65 per cent of your recommended daily intake. It's also packed full of essential amino acids.

309 CALORIES | 5G FAT | 1.5G SATURATES | 4G CARBS | 3G SUGAR | 0.4G SALT | 61G PROTEIN | 3G FIBRE

SERVES 2

1 egg

450g lean turkey mince

½ red onion, finely chopped

1 garlic clove, crushed

1 teaspoon dried crushed chillies

1.5cm cube fresh ginger, grated

a handful of coriander, finely chopped

4 nori (seaweed) sheets

4 medium asparagus, trimmed

1 jalapeno pepper, trimmed and sliced into wheels

1. Place the egg, turkey mince, onion, garlic, chilli, ginger and coriander in a bowl and mix together.

2. Lay a nori sheet, shiny side down, on the mat and lay a quarter of the turkey mix across the sheet in a thin layer, pressing down with a spoon or fork, but leaving the furthest edge clear.

3. Lay the asparagus down the middle of each sheet, then use the mat to roll the sushi up, applying gentle pressure to keep the roll tight. When you get to the far edge of the nori, dab it with a little water to seal it up. Repeat with the remaining nori sheets.

4. Place the rolls in a bamboo steamer set over a saucepan of boiling water, turn the heat down to low and steam for about 22 minutes.

5. Transfer the sushi to a chopping board and, using a sharp knife, trim the ends and then slice the long roll into half, and then half again. Serve each sushi with a slice of jalapeno pepper on top.

CRAB, DILL & ONION

138 CALORIES | 5G FAT | 1G SATURATES | 3.5G CARBS | 3G SUGAR | 1.2G SALT | 18G PROTEIN | 2.5G FIBRE

SERVES 2

1 x 180g tin white crab meat, drained

¼ red onion, finely chopped

1 tablespoon sesame seeds

1 tablespoon lemon juice

2 tablespoons chopped fresh dill

2 nori (seaweed) sheets

2 spring onions, trimmed and
   sliced lengthways

¼ cucumber, peeled and sliced
   lengthways into quarters

1. Place the crab, red onion, sesame seeds, lemon juice and dill in a bowl and mix together.

2. Lay a nori sheet, shiny side down, on the mat and spread half of the crab mix across the sheet in a thin layer, but leaving the furthest edge clear.

3. Lay the spring onion and cucumber down the middle of each sheet, then use the mat to roll the sushi up, applying gentle pressure to keep the roll tight.

4. When you get to the far edge of the nori, dab it with a little water to seal it up. Trim the ends with a sharp knife, then slice the long roll into half, and then half again. Repeat with the second nori sheet, then serve.

TUNA SALAD WITH WASABI

119 CALORIES | 0.8G FAT | 0G SATURATES | 3G CARBS | 2.5G SUGAR | 0.2G SALT | 24G PROTEIN | 2G FIBRE

SERVES 2

1 x 180g tin tuna in water, drained

1 teaspoon wasabi paste

¼ red onion, finely chopped

4–6 fresh basil leaves, finely sliced

2 nori (seaweed) sheets

1 tablespoon lemon juice

1 spring onion

¼ cucumber, peeled and sliced
   lengthways into quarters

1. Place the tuna, red onion, lemon juice, wasabi and basil in a bowl and mix together.

2. Lay a nori sheet, shiny side down, on the mat and spread half of the tuna mix across the sheet in a thin layer, but leaving the furthest edge clear.

3. Lay the spring onion and cucumber down the middle of each sheet, then use the mat to roll the sushi up, applying gentle pressure to keep the roll tight.

4. When you get to the far edge of the nori, dab it with a little water to seal it up. Trim the ends with a sharp knife, then slice the long roll into half, and then half again. Repeat with the second nori sheet, then serve.

SALMON & SESAME

346 CALORIES | 26G FAT | 4.5G SATURATES | 1.5G CARBS | 1.5G SUGAR | 0.5G SALT | 25G PROTEIN | 4.5G FIBRE

SERVES 2

200g salmon fillet

2 nori (seaweed) sheets

1 tablespoon sesame seeds

1 teaspoon sesame oil

200g spinach

1. Place the salmon fillet on a chopping board and, using a very sharp knife, slice lengthways into quarters.

2. Lay a nori sheet, shiny side down, on the mat and place 2 salmon slices lengthways, edge to edge. Sprinkle over half the sesame seeds and drizzle over half the sesame oil.

3. Wilt the spinach either in a bamboo steamer set over a pan of gently simmering water, then squeeze out the excess juices with a sheet of kitchen paper.

4. Line the spinach next to the salmon along the nori sheet, then then use the mat to roll the sushi up, applying gentle pressure to keep the roll tight.

5. When you get to the far edge, dab it with a little water to seal it up. Trim the ends with a sharp knife, then slice the long roll into half, and then half again. Repeat with the second nori sheet, then serve.

TIP Always ask the fishmonger if the salmon is fresh so you can have it raw. If you are worried about using raw salmon you can squeeze fresh lemon juice over the fish and let it cure for 3–4 minutes as this kills most bacteria.

SALMON SASHIMI

270 CALORIES | 17G FAT | 3G SATURATES | 4G CARBS | 3G SUGAR | 1.2G SALT | 24G PROTEIN | 1.7G FIBRE

SERVES 2

225g salmon fillet, chopped
   into cubes
½ white onion finely chopped
1 tablespoon coconut aminos
¼ red chilli, finely chopped
   (deseeded if you like)
juice of 1 lemon
2 nori (seaweed) sheets
¼ cucumber, peeled and sliced
   lengthways into quarters

1. Place the salmon, onion, coconut aminos, chilli and lemon juice in a bowl and mix together.

2. Lay a nori sheet, shiny side down, on the mat and spread half of the salmon mix across the sheet in a thin layer, but leaving the furthest edge clear.

3. Lay the cucumber down the middle of each sheet, then use the mat to roll the sushi up, applying gentle pressure to keep the roll tight.

4. When you get to the far edge of the nori, dab it with a little water to seal it up. Trim the ends with a sharp knife, then slice the long roll into half, and then half again. Repeat with the second nori sheet, then serve.

TUNA SASHIMI

368 CALORIES | 11.5G FAT | 2G SATURATES | 0.8G CARBS | 0.6G SUGAR | 0.6G SALT | 61G PROTEIN | 7G FIBRE

SERVES 2

450g tuna, finely cubed
¼ red onion, finely chopped
a handful of fresh coriander, roughly
   chopped
1 tablespoon sesame oil
1 tablespoon sesame seeds
¼ red chilli, finely chopped
1.5cm cube ginger, grated
¼ cucumber, finely chopped
wasabi paste (see page 68)
4 nori (seaweed) sheets

1. Place all the ingredients except the wasabi and seaweed in a bowl and mix well.

2. Lay a nori sheet, shiny side down, on the mat and draw a thin line of wasabi paste across the length of the sheet. Spread a quarter of the tuna mix across the sheet in a thin layer, leaving the furthest edge clear, and use the mat to roll the sushi up, applying gentle pressure to keep the roll tight.

3. When you get to the far edge of the nori, dab it with a little water to seal it up. Trim the ends with a sharp knife, then slice the long roll into half, and then half again. Repeat with the remaining nori sheets, then serve.

KOREAN BEEF TARTARE

I first tasted this staple Korean dish when I was in Seoul and it blew me away.
The traditional version does use a lot of soy sauce, which is not strictly a Paleo
ingredient. However, coconut aminos provide a very good soy sauce substitute
(see page 10) so try it and see what you think.

433 CALORIES | 17.5G FAT | 5G SATURATES | 14G CARBS | 11.5G SUGAR | 1G SALT | 54G PROTEIN | 1.5G FIBRE

SERVES 4

1 Asian (Nashi) pear, peeled,
   cored and sliced into
   thin strips

juice of ½ lemon

900g very lean beef (beef
   tenderloin is best and
   must be fresh)

3 garlic cloves, finely chopped

2 tablespoons sesame oil

1 tablespoon sesame seeds

3 tablespoons coconut aminos
   (see page 10)

2 tablespoons raw honey or
   maple syrup

2 chicory heads, leaves
   separated

a handful of flat-leaf parsley,
   finely chopped

1. Place the Asian pear in a small bowl and
   squeeze over the lemon juice to prevent it
   from discolouring, then place in the fridge.

2. Cut the beef tenderloin into very small pieces
   and place in a large bowl. If you find any fat,
   discard it. Add the garlic, sesame oil, sesame
   seeds and coconut aminos to the beef and
   mix well. Add the honey and mix again until
   thoroughly combined. Cover and refrigerate
   for at least 20 minutes but for no more than
   an hour.

3. When ready to serve, add the pear to the beef
   and mix again. Serve with a few chicory leaves
   and a scattering of parsley to garnish.

TIP I recommend that you use beef tenderloin for this recipe
and do make sure that the meat is very very fresh as you
are serving it raw.

OLIVE & TUNA TAPENADE

347 CALORIES | 20G FAT | 3G SATURATES | 15G CARBS | 14G SUGAR | 3.3G SALT | 22G PROTEIN | 11G FIBRE

SERVES 2

for the dip

1 x 170g tin pitted black olives

1 x 140g tin tuna in water, drained

1 tablespoon capers

1 tablespoon olive oil

1 garlic clove, peeled

juice of ½ lemon

½ white onion

a small handful of fresh basil (optional)

1 tablespoon Dijon mustard

for the crudités

300g carrots, peeled and cut into sticks

300g celery, cut into sticks

½ cucumber, cut into sticks

a bunch of radishes, topped and tailed and quartered

1. Simply place all the dip ingredients in a food processor (or alternatively use a hand-held electric blender) and whiz together for a few minutes, ensuring the ingredients are chopped but still nice and chunky (this is a tapenade, not a paste).

2. Serve as a dip with a selection of fresh, crunchy crudités.

SALMON TAPENADE

285 CALORIES | 12G FAT | 2G SATURATES | 15G CARBS | 13G SUGAR | 1.6G SALT | 25G PROTEIN | 8G FIBRE

SERVES 2

for the dip

1 x 180g tin salmon, drained

juice of 1 lemon

1 teaspoon capers

a small handful of fresh basil leaves

1 tablespoon sun-dried tomatoes in olive oil

4–6 cherry tomatoes

½ small red chilli or 1 teaspoon dried crushed chillies

¼ red onion, finely chopped

a few chives, chopped (for garnish)

for the crudités

300g carrots, peeled and cut into sticks

300g celery, cut into sticks

½ cucumber, cut into sticks

a bunch of radishes, topped and tailed and quartered

1. Place all the dip ingredients except the red onion and chives in a food processor and whiz until it is a nice chunky blend, then transfer to a bowl.

2. Add the red onion and stir through and serve with crudités of your choice with a sprinkle of cut chives.

PAN-FRIED CALAMARI
WITH GINGER & LIME

When we think of calamari we often think of deep-fried guilty pleasure. However, with this recipe you can skip the guilt and just focus on the pleasure. Squid is also very inexpensive, plus it's full of protein and essential vitamins and minerals (especially calcium).

212 CALORIES | 7G FAT | 1.5G SATURATES | 1G CARBS | 1G SUGAR | 0.6G SALT | 36G PROTEIN | 1.5G

SERVES 4

1 tablespoon olive oil

900g squid, cleaned and thinly sliced

sea salt and freshly ground black pepper

zest of ½ lime

juice of 1 lime

2 garlic cloves, crushed

2.5cm cube of fresh ginger, peeled and grated

400g rocket leaves

1 lemon, quartered

1. Place the olive oil in a large non-stick frying pan and place over a very high heat. When hot, add the squid, season and stir-fry for 3–4 minutes, then transfer to a bowl, being sure to include all the crispy pan scrapings and set aside.

2. In a bowl, mix together the lime zest, lime juice, garlic and ginger.

3. Arrange a pile of rocket on a plate, place the calamari on top with the lemon wedges, then pour over the citrusy sauce.

TIP You can add a little extra virgin olive oil when you plate the dish, and a twist of freshly ground black pepper.

SALMON & SCALLOP CEVICHE

This is such a healthy, fresh-tasting dish and it looks so beautiful arranged on one big serving plate – a dinner party starter that's perfect for sharing. Feel free to add a little wasabi, if you like.

267 CALORIES | 16.5G FAT | 3G SATURATES | 2G CARBS | 1.5G SUGAR | 0.3G SALT | 27G PROTEIN | 0.7G

SERVES 4

350g skinless salmon fillet

8 large scallops

juice of ½ lime

1 tablespoon olive oil

1 small red chilli, deseeded and finely chopped

½ dozen chives, finely chopped

4 shallots, finely chopped

sea salt and freshly ground black pepper

wasabi paste, optional

1. Using a very sharp knife, cut the salmon and scallops into very thin slices.

2. Arrange the fish and seafood on a plate and squeeze over the lime juice, then drizzle with olive oil.

3. Place the chilli, chives and shallots in a bowl and mix together well, then scatter over the ceviche on the plate. Season with salt and pepper and serve immediately with a little wasabi if you like.

TIP If you are a little concerned about cooking with raw fish at home, don't be put off by this recipe as the acidity of the lime juice cures the salmon and scallops, which eliminates any bacteria. However, it is always best to use the freshest fish and seafood you can find and I recommend asking your fishmonger so you are absolutely sure.

COURGETTE SPAGHETTI
WITH BACON & BASIL

This recipe gives you the texture and flavour of spaghetti but without the carbs –
genius! And if you want to make the best, long courgette spaghetti ribbons it's a
good idea to invest in a julienne peeler or a fancy spiralising gadget.

208 CALORIES | 17G FAT | 3.5G SATURATES | 3G CARBS | 3G SUGAR | 1.1G SALT | 9.5G PROTEIN | 2G FIBRE

SERVES 4 AS A SNACK OR SIDE DISH TO ANY MAIN MEAL

4 courgettes

2 tablespoons olive oil

6 rashers back bacon,
    trimmed of all fat and
    thinly sliced

1 garlic clove, crushed

40g sun-dried tomatoes
    in olive oil, drained and
    sliced into strips

1 small red chilli, finely
    chopped

1 tablespoon pine nuts

a handful of fresh basil,
    thinly shredded

1. First make your spaghetti by either grating the
   courgettes at an angle on the largest side of
   a cheese grater or using a hand-held julienne
   peeler or spiraliser.

2. Place 1 tablespoon olive oil in a large non-stick
   frying pan over a high heat and stir-fry the
   courgettes for 3 minutes. Add the bacon to the
   pan and sauté for a few minutes until cooked.
   Reduce the heat to medium.

3. Add the garlic, sun-dried tomatoes, chilli, pine
   nuts and the remaining olive oil to the pan.
   Toss for a few minutes, then take off the heat.

4. Divide the spaghetti between four bowls,
   scatter over the basil and serve immediately.

TIP To prevent the courgette spaghetti from getting mushy,
either cook it in a very large pan or do it in two batches.

TUNA TATAKI

Nothing is more Paleo than a beautiful plate of fresh, raw fish. I also love making this with salmon, and sometimes, instead of shredding the seaweed, I enclose the fish in a nori wrap.

421 CALORIES | 16G FAT | 3.5G SATURATES | 2.5G CARBS | 1.5G SUGAR | 0.9G SALT | 65G PROTEIN | 3G FIBRE

SERVES 4

1kg very fresh tuna

½ small red onion, finely chopped

a handful of fresh coriander leaves, finely chopped

1 tablespoon coconut aminos

1 tablespoon sesame seeds

2.5cm cube fresh ginger, grated

1 tablespoon sesame oil

1 red bird's eye chilli, finely chopped

1 sheet of seaweed, shredded

1 large avocado, diced

1. With a very sharp knife, on a very clean chopping board, shave the tuna into long, thin slices, discarding any sinew. Transfer to a bowl.

2. Add all the remaining ingredients to the bowl and mix well. Finally stir through the avocado and divide between four plates.

3. Serve with an extra scatter of coriander.

TIP The B vitamins in tuna help to build and maintain red blood cells and increase energy. They also increase the rate of metabolism, strengthen the immune system and keep the skin healthy.

BUFFALO CHICKEN STRIPS

If you have ever been to the United States then I bet you have had Buffalo wings. They are often served as starters or bar food and, more often than not, they're deep-fried and served with blue cheese dip – delicious, but perhaps not one of the healthiest foods out there! My version, however, is healthy and sacrifices none of the flavour. You really do have to use Frank's sauce for authenticity but as it contains a few ingredients that aren't strictly Paleo, keep this for a weekend, or alternatively make up your own Hot Wings Sauce using the recipe below.

377 CALORIES | 14G FAT | 8G SATURATES | 2G CARBS | 2G SUGAR | 0.9G SALT | 60G PROTEIN | 1G FIBRE

SERVES 4

4 x 250g skinless chicken breasts, cut into strips

1 tablespoon olive oil

sea salt and freshly ground black pepper

110ml buffalo sauce (Frank's Hot Wings Sauce is the one to use, or see the Tip below)

6 large celery sticks, trimmed and finely sliced

4 spring onions, finely sliced

1. Rub the chicken strips all over with the olive oil and season lightly.

2. Place a large non-stick frying pan over a high heat and cook the chicken for about 3–4 minutes on each side. Add the buffalo sauce, then quickly take off the heat (it will bubble fast and the pepper will hit the air) and toss the pan to evenly coat the chicken.

3. Serve the chicken over the celery and scatter the spring onion on top.

TIP As with so many shop-bought condiments, Hot Wing's Sauce doesn't quite meet the strict Paleo criteria, so here's a recipe you can make up at home: Melt 3 tablespoons coconut oil in a saucepan over a low heat, then whisk in 3–4 tablespoons hot sauce, 1 teaspoon garlic powder, 1 teaspoon paprika, 1 tablespoon lemon juice, 1 tablespoon white wine vinegar and lightly season with salt and pepper.

MEATLOAF

Now that I've been living in the US for over a decade, I've lost count of the incredibly delicious meatloaves that I've tasted over the years. As it's such a classic and staple dish here and as it's the perfect solution for when you're catering for large numbers, I felt I had to include my own Paleo version.

673 CALORIES | 32G FAT | 10G SATURATES | 3.5G CARBS | 2.5G SUGAR | 0.4G SALT | 34G PROTEIN | 1G FIBRE

SERVES 8

150g salad leaves, to serve

for the meatloaf

1.2kg lean beef mince

1 egg and 1 egg white

½ white onion, finely chopped

3 garlic cloves, crushed

2 tablespoons homemade Hot Wings Sauce (see page 75)

2–3 tablespoons freshly chopped parsley

2 tablespoons almond flour

2 tablespoons tomato purée

2 tablespoons homemade tomato ketchup (see page 26)

50g roughly chopped sun-dried tomatoes

1. Preheat the oven to 180°C/gas mark 4.

2. Place all the meatloaf ingredients in a large bowl and, using your hands, mix everything together until thoroughly combined.

3. Take a 1kg loaf tin and spray with a little olive oil.

4. Tip the meatloaf mixture into the tin so that it fills every corner, level off the top and cover with foil. Cook in the oven for 30 minutes, then remove the foil and bake for a further 20 minutes until beautifully browned on top.

5. Serve hot with something bright and green, like salad.

TIP A pan of hot water in the oven, under the tin, will stop the top of the loaf from cracking.

SOUPS & SALADS

TOMATO SOUP

This is a great example of how you only need a few ingredients to make a fantastic soup and how there's no need for traditional starchy thickeners like potato.

216 CALORIES | 11G FAT | 1.5G SATURATES | 21G CARBS | 20G SUGAR | 1G SALT | 4.5G PROTEIN | 7G FIBRE

SERVES 4

1 tablespoon olive oil

1kg fresh tomatoes

250ml passata

250ml vegetable stock

60g sun-dried tomatoes in olive oil

1 teaspoon cracked pepper

½ teaspoon chilli powder

2 garlic cloves, crushed

a handful of fresh basil leaves, shredded

1. Heat the olive oil in a large saucepan over a medium heat and sauté the tomatoes for 2–3 minutes.

2. Add the passata, stock and sun-dried tomatoes and stir to combine, then add the pepper, chilli and garlic and stir some more.

3. Bring to the boil, cover and simmer for 15 minutes, then add half the basil, stir and remove from the heat.

4. Using a liquidiser or hand-held blender, blend the soup until smooth, then pour the soup into a saucepan, season with black pepper and heat until barely simmering.

5. Remove from the heat, divide between four serving bowls and garnish with the remaining fresh basil.

BROCCOLI SOUP

Many soup recipes use potato as the starch works as a great thickening agent. However, there are ingredients, like watercress or broccoli, which do the same thing without the starch and so are perfect for Paleo.

116 CALORIES | 4G FAT | 0.7G SATURATES | 7.5G CARBS | 5.5G SUGAR | 1.5G SALT | 8G PROTEIN | 8G FIBRE

SERVES 4

1 tablespoon olive oil

1 medium white onion, roughly chopped

1 medium leek, trimmed and roughly chopped

3 garlic cloves, crushed

600g fresh broccoli florets

1 litre vegetable stock

freshly ground black pepper

a handful of basil leaves, torn

1. Heat the oil in a large saucepan over a medium heat and sweat the onion for 2–3 minutes.

2. Add the leeks and garlic and cook for a further minute, then add the broccoli and stock and stir to combine. Turn up the heat to bring to the boil, then reduce to a simmer and cook for 30 minutes. Set aside to cool.

3. Using a liquidiser or hand-held blender, blend the vegetables until smooth.

4. Pour the soup back into the saucepan, season with black pepper, then heat until barely simmering.

5. Remove from the heat, divide between four serving bowls and garnish with a scattering of basil leaves.

TIP If you like a little more texture in your soup, only roughly blend the vegetables so it's not completely smooth.

CAULIFLOWER SOUP

Cauliflower is a great low-carb alternative to using potato as a thickening agent.
Add more stock to this one if you prefer a thinner, more purée-like consistency.

126 CALORIES | 6G FAT | 1G SATURATES | 10G CARBS | 7G SUGAR | 0.1G SALT | 5G PROTEIN | 4G FIBRE

SERVES 4

2 tablespoons olive oil

1 medium white onion, roughly chopped

2 garlic cloves, crushed

1 cauliflower, broken into florets

60ml vegetable stock

freshly ground black pepper

a handful of flat-leaf parsley, finely chopped

1. Heat the olive oil in a large saucepan over a medium heat and sweat the onion for 1–2 minutes.

2. Add the garlic and cauliflower and stir to cook for a minute, then cover with stock, bring to the boil and simmer for 40 minutes. Remove from the heat.

3. Using a liquidiser or hand-held blender, blend until smooth.

4. Pour the soup back into the saucepan, season with black pepper, then heat until barely simmering.

5. Remove from the heat, divide between your serving bowls and garnish with a sprinkling of parsley.

TIP I love cauliflower as its mild flavour makes it incredibly versatile. Use it as a thickening agent in soups or even cook it until soft and then mash as a wonderful low-carb alternative to mashed potato.

GAZPACHO

This traditional Spanish soup is always served chilled and makes a deliciously refreshing meal in hot weather. Try it in little glasses with prawns for a summer party canapé.

113 CALORIES | 6G FAT | 0.9G SATURATES | 11G CARBS | 10G SUGAR | TRACE SALT | 2G PROTEIN | 0.4G FIBRE

SERVES 4

1kg tomatoes, roughly chopped

1 small white onion, roughly chopped

1 garlic clove, crushed

1 red pepper, deseeded and finely chopped

2 tablespoons olive oil

2 tablespoons white wine vinegar

½ cucumber, halved, seeds scooped out and finely chopped

sea salt and freshly ground black pepper

a handful of flat-leaf parsley, finely chopped

1. Place the tomatoes, onion, garlic, pepper, olive oil and vinegar in a blender and pulse until smooth. Stir in the cucumber, season to taste, then place in the refrigerator for at least an hour.

2. Serve with a scattering of fresh parsley.

TIP This soup also makes a great base for a seafood sauce or a simple fish stew.

VEGETABLE COMFORT SOUP
WITH MEATBALLS

This is my favourite comfort soup for rainy days. It's what I make when I am home all day and feel just plain hungry and however much I eat, it always leaves me feeling satisfied and never like I've overindulged!

293 CALORIES | 7G FAT | 1.7G SATURATES | 10G CARBS | 8G SUGAR | 1G SALT | 46G PROTEIN | 5G FIBRE

SERVES 4

1 tablespoon olive oil

1 medium onion, finely chopped

225g carrots, peeled and chopped into small cubes

1 leek, finely chopped

1.75 litres chicken stock

1 teaspoon fresh cracked pepper

200g spinach

for the meatballs

450g chicken mince

1 small red chilli, finely chopped

½ red onion, finely chopped

1 egg

1 tablespoon tomato purée

4 garlic cloves, crushed

1 tablespoon dried basil

1. First make the meatballs: Place the chicken mince, chilli, red onion, egg, tomato purée, half the garlic and half the dried basil in a large bowl and use your hands to mix together well.

2. Divide the mixture into tablespoon-size scoops and roll into balls. Place on a large plate.

3. Heat the oil in a large stockpot and sauté the onion for 2 minutes. Add the carrots, leek and the remaining basil and garlic and sauté for a further minute, then add the stock and pepper and bring to the boil.

4. Add the meatballs to the stockpot, cover and cook for 15 minutes. Add the spinach, cover again and cook for a further 5 minutes.

5. Remove the pan from the heat, divide between four serving bowls and serve immediately.

TIP If you want a little more flavour add a tablespoon of homemade pesto.

GRILLED CHICKEN SALAD
WITH FRUIT & NUTS

I love including fruit in a salad. It provides such great colour and adds a lovely fresh sweetness that works so well with peppery greens and toasted nuts.

247 CALORIES | 8G FAT | 1G SATURATES | 12G CARBS | 12G SUGAR | 0.4G SALT | 30G PROTEIN | 2.5G FIBRE

SERVES 4

4 x 115g boneless skinless chicken breast halves

for the marinade
120ml fresh lime juice
2 tablespoons honey
4 teaspoons olive oil
½ teaspoon salt
½ teaspoon pepper

for the salad
150g mixed salad greens
150g cubed seedless watermelon
150g fresh blueberries
1 medium yellow pepper, cubed
2 tablespoons chopped walnuts, toasted

1. First make the marinade: In a small bowl, combine the lime juice, honey, oil, salt and pepper and whisk together.

2. Pour two-thirds of the marinade (about 115ml) into a large resealable plastic bag. Place the chicken in the bag, seal it and, ensuring all the meat is covered with the marinade, place in the fridge for at least 1 hour. Set the remaining marinade mixture aside for a dressing.

3. When you are ready to cook the chicken, heat a griddle pan over a medium heat. When hot, drain and discard the marinade and cook the chicken in the hot pan for 4–7 minutes on each side.

4. In a large bowl, combine the salad greens, watermelon, blueberries and yellow pepper, add the reserved dressing and toss to coat. Divide among four serving plates.

5. Using a sharp knife, slice each chicken breast into four pieces and divide these pieces between the four plates, together with the walnuts. Serve immediately.

TIP Blueberries are loaded with fibre, which will keep you feeling full for longer, and provide you with almost 25% of your daily value of vitamin C.

AVOCADO CHICKEN SALAD

This salad is great for a busy midweek supper as it only takes minutes to prepare.

386 CALORIES | 20G FAT | 3.5G SATURATES | 12G CARBS | 10G SUGAR | 0.2G SALT | 39G PROTEIN | 4G FIBRE

SERVES 4

4 skinless chicken breasts

1 tablespoon olive oil

1 large ripe avocado, peeled and destoned (or 2 smaller avocados)

a squeeze of lime

1 green apple, chopped into small cubes

55g red seedless grapes, halved

2 tablespoons chopped walnuts

2 tablespoons dried cranberries or raisins

a handful of coriander, finely chopped

juice of 1 lime

sea salt, to taste

2 little gems, leaves separated

1. Preheat the grill to medium. Rub the chicken all over with a little olive oil and grill for 4–5 minutes on each side until lightly charred and cooked through.

2. Place the avocado in a large bowl and mash to a chunky/ creamy consistency with a squeeze of lime.

3. Place the apple, grapes, walnuts, cranberries or raisins, and coriander in a bowl and toss to combine. Add the lime juice and the salt to taste and toss again.

4. Place a few lettuce leaves on each plate and spoon over the fruit and nut mix. Serve with the chicken (sliced if you prefer) and a large spoonful of creamy avocado on the side.

TIP To keep this salad from turning brown, try leaving the stone from the avocado in the mixture until ready to serve. And if you'd like something with a more mayo-like consistency, try the avocado mayo recipe on page 48.

CHICKEN LIVER SALAD
WITH FRIED ONIONS

This dish is deservedly a classic of French cuisine and makes a fantastically simple mid-week supper. Chicken liver also couldn't be better for you – it's inexpensive, full of protein and really delicious. The trick is to fry it in a hot pan for just a couple of minutes on each side. Don't overcook it!

174 CALORIES | 8.5G FAT | 1.5G SATURATES | 3G CARBS | 2.5G SUGAR | 0.4G SALT | 20G PROTEIN | 2.5G FIBRE

SERVES 4

2 tablespoons olive oil

1 red onion, finely sliced

400g chicken livers

200g spinach

100g watercress

1 teaspoon balsamic vinegar

English mustard, to serve

1. Heat 1 tablespoon of oil in a large non-stick sauté pan over a medium-high heat and fry the onion for 3–4 minutes until nicely browned. Transfer to a plate and set aside.

2. Turn the heat up to high, add ½ tablespoon olive oil to the pan and cook the chicken livers for 2 minutes on each side until they are a lovely nutty brown on the outside and pink and tender in the middle. Transfer to a plate and set aside.

3. In a large bowl, mix together the spinach and watercress and toss with remaining olive oil and a little balsamic vinegar.

4. Divide the dressed salad leaves between four plates, arrange the chicken livers on top and scatter with the red onion. Drizzle any remaining juice from the pan over the meat and serve with a spoonful of English mustard.

TIP This dish is an iron-rich feast as the liver, watercress and spinach all contain huge amounts of this essential mineral – great for times when you feel weak, tired and especially run down.

GRILLED CHICKEN SALAD
WITH ROASTED TOMATOES & POACHED EGG

I just love this protein-rich salad. It's so easy to make and yet so satisfying, plus the roasted tomatoes add a really delicious sweetness that complements the chicken and egg perfectly.

456 CALORIES | 32G FAT | 5.5G SATURATES | 4G CARBS | 3.5G SUGAR | 0.9G SALT | 37G PROTEIN | 1.7G FIBRE

SERVES 4

for the marinade and dressing

60ml sherry vinegar or
   champagne vinegar

1 tablespoon Dijon mustard

1 tablespoon white truffle oil

1 teaspoon chopped fresh
   thyme leaves

2 garlic cloves, finely chopped

½ teaspoon sea salt

¼ teaspoon freshly ground
   black pepper

120ml extra virgin olive oil

for the salad

4 x 115g boneless skinless
   chicken breast halves

300g cherry tomatoes,
   cut in half

4 eggs

2 teaspoons vinegar (any
   flavour)

200g salad greens (a mix
   of round lettuce, frisée,
   spinach, etc.)

1. Preheat the oven to 220°C/gas mark 7.

2. In a small bowl, combine the vinegar, mustard, truffle oil, thyme, garlic and salt and pepper, then slowly whisk in the extra virgin olive oil. Pour about half of the mixture into a large resealable plastic bag and reserve the rest. Place the chicken in the marinade, seal the bag and turn to coat the meat thoroughly, then refrigerate for at least 1 hour or overnight.

3. In a large bowl, toss the tomatoes in 2 tablespoons of the reserved dressing, then spread them out over a baking sheet and roast in the oven for 15–20 minutes until slightly shrivelled. Set aside to cool.

4. Remove the chicken from the bag and drain and discard the marinade. Place a griddle pan over a high heat and cook the chicken for 4–7 minutes on each side or until cooked through. Set aside to cool slightly, then slice at a diagonal.

5. Meanwhile, bring a saucepan of water to a simmer on the hob. Add the vinegar and slide in each freshly cracked egg. Poach for about 3 minutes or to your desired doneness, then remove with a slotted spoon and drain on kitchen paper.

6. In a large bowl, combine the salad greens with the remaining dressing and toss to coat. Divide between four serving plates and top with the roasted tomatoes and sliced chicken and finish with a freshly poached egg.

GRILLED SALMON SALAD

Orange and salmon are a lovely combination in this simple, fresh and zesty salad.

794 CALORIES | 60G FAT | 9G SATURATES | 23G CARBS | 22G SUGAR | 1.7G SALT | 37G PROTEIN | 9G FIBRE

SERVES 2

10 asparagus spears, trimmed

2 x 150g salmon fillets

4 teaspoons olive oil

sea salt and freshly ground
  black pepper

120g salad leaves

120g destoned kalamata
  olives, sliced in half

1 orange, peeled and
  segmented

½ red onion, thinly sliced

for the orange vinaigrette

½ large orange

2 teaspoons finely chopped
  shallots

1 teaspoon raw honey

1 teaspoon seasoned rice
  vinegar

60ml sunflower oil

1 teaspoon extra virgin
  olive oil

sea salt and freshly ground
  black pepper

¼ teaspoon orange oil
  (optional)

1. First make the vinaigrette: Zest the orange and squeeze the juice into a small bowl. Add the zest, shallots, honey and rice vinegar to the orange juice and whisk together. Next add the sunflower oil and olive oil slowly, in a steady stream, while constantly whisking. Add the salt, pepper and orange oil and whisk again until combined.

2. Preheat the grill to high. Bring a saucepan of water to the boil and cook the asparagus for 30 seconds, then drain and place under cold running water to stop the cooking process, and set aside.

3. Rub the salmon fillets all over with half the olive oil and season lightly. Place under the grill for 5–10 minutes on each side, or until done to your liking. Set aside.

4. Place the salad leaves, olives, orange, onion and half of the vinaigrette in a large bowl and toss to combine.

5. Toss the asparagus in the remaining oil and season lightly, then place under the hot grill for about 3 minutes until lightly charred.

6. Divide the salad between two plates, place the asparagus and salmon on top and drizzle the remaining dressing over the salmon. Serve immediately.

TIP Boyajian Orange Oil is available at speciality food stores. It is very strong so only a small amount is needed.

SALMON, SWEETCORN & AVOCADO SALAD

I love the textures in this salad. Try and use the freshest sweetcorn you can find as then there is no need to cook it and it's deliciously sweet and crunchy.

590 CALORIES | 43G FAT | 7.5G SATURATES | 11G CARBS | 4G SUGAR | 0.2G SALT | 37G PROTEIN | 4.5G FIBRE

SERVES 4

for the salad

4 ears fresh sweetcorn, kernels removed from cob

10 cherry tomatoes, halved

1 small avocado, peeled, destoned and diced

½ red onion, finely chopped

a large handful of fresh coriander, finely chopped

2 tablespoons extra virgin olive oil

2 tablespoons champagne vinegar

2 tablespoons red wine vinegar

for the salmon

4 x 160g boneless, skinless salmon fillets

½ tablespoon extra virgin olive oil

sea salt and freshly ground black pepper

½ lemon

1. Preheat the grill to medium.

2. Place the corn, tomatoes, avocado, onion, coriander, oil and vinegars in a large bowl and toss gently to combine. Set aside.

3. Lightly brush each salmon fillet all over with a little olive oil and season to taste. Place the fillets under the grill and cook for about 4–5 minutes on each side.

4. Fork the cooked salmon into small chunks so you can see the juicy pink flesh and squeeze over a little lemon.

5. Divide the salad between four serving bowls, lay the salmon on top and serve immediately while the fish is still warm.

VENISON & POMEGRANATE SALAD

Venison is a very lean meat so is excellent if you're watching your weight. It's best served on the rare side so make sure you only cook with very fresh meat.

285 CALORIES | 6G FAT | 2G SATURATES | 20G CARBS | 19G SUGAR | 0.8G SALT | 36G PROTEIN | 4G FIBRE

SERVES 4

a drizzle of olive oil

sea salt and crushed black pepper

2 x 300g venison steaks

400g mixed salad leaves

½ red onion, finely sliced

1 orange, peeled and sliced into segments

150g pomegranate seeds

for the balsamic vinaigrette

100ml balsamic vinegar

juice of ½ large lemon

2 tablespoons Dijon mustard

1 garlic clove, crushed

1 teaspoon dried basil

1 tablespoon maple syrup

1. Drizzle a little oil into a large non-stick frying pan, lightly season the venison and then sear over a high heat for about 3 minutes on each side. Turn off the heat and let the meat rest in the pan for 5 minutes, then turn and let it rest for another few minutes.

2. Meanwhile, make the dressing. Place all the ingredients in a jar and shake well.

3. Place the salad leaves in a large bowl and toss together with a little dressing. Divide the salad between four plates, add the red onion and orange segments and sprinkle over the pomegranate seeds.

4. Place the rested meat on a chopping board and, with a sharp knife, slice the steaks thinly. Arrange the slices over the salad and serve immediately.

TIP Venison is a great healthy eating choice – it has more protein than any other red meat and contains even more iron than beef, so is good for energy levels. Also, because of all the wild and pasture food that deer graze on, the small amount of fat in venison is generally high in conjugated linoleic acid, which is thought to protect against heart disease and cancer.

MAIN MEALS

BUTTERNUT SQUASH CURRY

I try not to cook with large amounts of butternut squash as it's quite high in carbs.
However, as there's no protein in this curry, you'll need the carbs to fill you up,
plus I love the way the squash and coconut milk cook down and flavour each other
– it's a true Thai classic.

269 CALORIES | 15G FAT | 7G SATURATES | 22G CARBS | 14G SUGAR | 0.3G SALT | 7G PROTEIN | 8G FIBRE

SERVES 4

1 medium butternut squash, peeled, deseeded and chopped into 5cm pieces

2 tablespoons olive oil

1 small onion, finely chopped

4 courgettes, sliced lengthways, then quartered

2 teaspoons Thai red curry paste

2.5cm cube fresh ginger, grated

1 x 400ml tin light coconut milk

200g fresh spinach

a handful of fresh coriander, finely chopped

1. Preheat the oven to 200°C/gas mark 6.

2. Place the butternut squash in a roasting tin, drizzle with a tablespoon of oil and toss to coat, then roast in the oven for 30 minutes.

3. Heat the remaining olive oil in a large saucepan over a high heat and cook the onion for 2 minutes until translucent. Add the courgettes and cook for a further 3 minutes, then lower the heat to medium, add the butternut squash, stir together and cook for a few more minutes.

4. Add the curry paste and ginger and stir to coat, then add the coconut milk and cook, covered for 5 minutes.

5. Add the spinach, stir and cook for a further few minutes, then garnish with a scattering of coriander and serve immediately.

TIP Ginger is a great spice to cook with as it boosts the metabolism and has been shown to increase thermogenesis in the body, where your body burns stored fat to create heat. Research shows that it can boost your metabolism by up to 5 per cent, and increase fat burning by up to 16 per cent.

AUBERGINE LASAGNE

This is a delicious, healthy pasta-free lasagne. You can layer the aubergine or roll it up like a cannelloni and either way is perfect for a satisfying Italian-style feast.

318 CALORIES | 20G FAT | 7G SATURATES | 8G CARBS | 7G SUGAR | 0.1G SALT | 24G PROTEIN | 7G FIBRE

SERVES 4

2 tablespoons olive oil

2 large aubergines, cut into 1cm slices

½ white onion, finely chopped

450g lean beef mince

2 garlic cloves, crushed

1 tablespoon sun-dried tomato purée

2 tablespoons tomato purée

a handful of fresh basil, shredded

30ml vegetable stock

150g salad leaves, to serve

1. Preheat the oven to 180°C/gas mark 6.

2. Heat 1 tablespoon of olive oil in a large non-stick griddle pan over a high heat and grill the aubergine slices for a couple of minutes on each side until nice and brown (you may have to do this in batches as it's important not to crowd the pan).

3. Heat the remaining olive oil in a large sauté pan and cook the onion over a medium to high heat for 2-3 minutes.

4. Add the mince and sauté for 2-3 minutes to brown, then add the garlic, tomato purées, a tablespoon of basil and the stock, cover and simmer for 3–4 minutes.

5. Take a lasagne dish and line the base with aubergine slices. Spoon over a third of the bolognese sauce, then cover with a layer of aubergine slices and repeat until all the sauce is used up, finishing with a layer of aubergine on top.

6. Cover with foil and place in the oven for 15–18 minutes. If you prefer a crunchy top, remove the foil at the end, spray with a little extra oil and place under the grill for 2–3 minutes.

7. Serve with a scattering of fresh basil and a bright, fresh green salad.

DINNER FOR A KING

This is the dinner I cook when I want to indulge myself and my family and friends.
I often add lobster if it's a special occasion or swap the tinned crab for fresh, and
scallops make a great addition too.

486 CALORIES | 29G FAT | 7G SATURATES | 2.5G CARBS | 2G SUGAR | 6G SALT | 52G PROTEIN | 3G FIBRE

SERVES 4

4–6 shallots, finely chopped

1 tablespoon chopped fresh
    dill

200g tinned white crab meat

200g rocket

600g Scottish smoked salmon

1 avocado, peeled, destoned
    and sliced

2 hard-boiled eggs, quartered

50g salmon caviar (roe)

sea salt and freshly ground
    black pepper

1 lemon, quartered

1. In a small mixing bowl, toss together the
   shallots, dill and crab meat and set aside.

2. Divide the rocket between four serving plates
   and top with the smoked salmon, avocado
   and two egg quarters, then spoon over the
   salmon caviar.

3. Add the crab meat mixture to the plate, season
   to taste and finish with a squeeze of lemon.
   Serve immediately.

TIP Fish eggs (also known as roe) are generally associated
with a fancy caviar canapé and are therefore very
overlooked as a kitchen ingredient, which is a shame as they
don't need to cost the earth (especially salmon or carp roe),
plus they're full of micro-nutrients and omega-3 fatty acids
and, most importantly, they're very tasty. The best way to
ensure quality is to buy fresh from your local fishmonger.
Roe in a jar or a can is often full of preservatives so read
the label carefully.

STUFFED SQUID
WITH PRAWNS

This recipe works well with both large and baby squid, although the former are quite a bit easier to fill!

565 CALORIES | 26G FAT | 5G SATURATES | 4G CARBS | 4G SUGAR | 2.6G SALT | 78G PROTEIN | 1G FIBRE

SERVES 4

1kg fresh squid, cleaned

450g skinless salmon fillet

340g shelled raw prawns, (large if possible)

juice of ½ lemon

1 egg

1 tablespoon coconut aminos

1 garlic clove, crushed

a handful of fresh coriander

freshly ground black pepper

1 x 400g tin chopped tomatoes

150ml vegetable or fish stock

1 tablespoon olive oil

1. First prepare the squid: Remove the tentacles and reserve. Pull away the wings, remove the head, and empty the main tube of cartilage and slime. Pull or cut away the eyes and beak, and remove anything else that feels hard or slimy from the tentacles. Discard everything but the cleaned tentacles and main body tube. Wash well and dry.

2. To make the filling, place the salmon, prawns, lemon juice, egg, coconut aminos, garlic and coriander and purée until smooth.

3. Fill each piece of squid to about two-thirds full and secure the end with a wooden cocktail stick. Season with black pepper and reserve until ready to cook.

4. Place the tomatoes and stock in a wide, deep sauté pan over a medium heat and bring to a low simmer, stirring to combine.

5. Heat the oil in another non-stick pan over a moderate heat and cook the squid for 2 minutes on each side.

6. Transfer the squid to the pan with the tomato sauce and cook, covered, over a medium to low heat for about 12–15 minutes. Turn half way through cooking time.

7. Serve the squid with a ladleful of tomato sauce and some extra coriander scattered on top.

GARLIC PRAWNS
WITH PAK CHOI

For this dish, the bigger the prawn the better. Tiger prawns from South East Asia are the largest and in my opinion the best tasting.

228 CALORIES | 4.5G FAT | 0.8G SATURATES | 3.5G CARBS | 2G SUGAR | 1.6G SALT | 42G PROTEIN | 3G FIBRE

SERVES 4

900g large raw tiger prawns

1 tablespoon olive oil

juice of ½ lemon

4 garlic cloves, finely chopped

1 tablespoon coconut aminos

6 heads pak choi, leaves separated

a handful of flat-leaf parsley, finely chopped

1. Keep the head on each prawn but peel the body and devein it by slicing through the back. Take out the dark line and discard it.

2. Spray a large non-stick sauté pan with a little olive oil, place on a high heat and cook the prawns for 2–3 minutes on each side, depending on how big they are.

3. Add the lemon juice, 2 garlic cloves and soy sauce, then take off the heat and stir fry for a minute while the pan is still hot. Leave to stand.

4. In another pan, heat 1 tablespoon olive oil and, when hot, stir-fry the pak choi for about 3–5 minutes. Add the remaining garlic, then cook for a further minute.

5. Serve the prawns with the pak choi, a scattering of parsley and a fresh squeeze of lemon.

TIP I recommend you keep the heads of the prawns on for cooking as there is so much flavour there. You can eat them too if you like – they are tasty – but it's up to you!

PAD THAI

This is the closest you can get to the flavours of a Pad Thai on the Paleo diet but it's a pretty good approximation – true comfort food at it's best!

129 CALORIES | 5G FAT | 1G SATURATES | 6G CARBS | 4G SUGAR | 0.8G SALT | 14G PROTEIN | 3G FIBRE

- -

SERVES 4

olive oil spray, for cooking

3 courgettes, sliced into matchsticks

a large handful of coriander leaves, finely chopped

2 spring onions, finely chopped

100g beansprouts

12 tiger prawns, peeled and deveined

25g cashews, to garnish

for the marinade

1 teaspoon fish sauce

juice of ½ lemon

1 teaspoon chilli powder

1 teaspoon maple syrup

1. First make the marinade: In a large bowl, mix together the fish sauce, lemon juice, chilli powder and maple syrup and set aside.

2. Heat a large non-stick wok over a high heat, spray with olive oil and sauté the courgettes for 2 minutes.

3. Remove the courgettes from the pan and add to the marinade. Stir to mix, then add the coriander, spring onions and bean sprouts.

4. Meanwhile, spray the wok again with a little oil and sauté the prawns for 2 minutes on each side until cooked through.

5. Divide the vegetables between four serving plates and scatter the prawns on top. Garnish with the cashews and serve.

- -

TIP Fish sauce is made from fermenting tiny fish, such as anchovies, in brine and then preserving the liquid so it should contain only two Paleo-friendly ingredients – fish and salt. However, check the labels and avoid any products with unnecessary extras such as hydrolysed wheat protein and fructose! Red Boat Fish Sauce is a good brand to look for.

GRILLED SWORDFISH
WITH MANGO SALSA

Swordfish is a lovely meaty fish that holds up really well to high heat so is the perfect choice for a barbecue. Try this dish with tuna and salmon as an alternative too.

326 CALORIES | 12G FAT | 2.5G SATURATES | 11G CARBS | 11G SUGAR | 0.7G SALT | 42G PROTEIN | 4G FIBRE

SERVES 4

4 x 220g swordfish steaks (about 2cm thick)

sea salt and freshly ground black pepper

1 tablespoon olive oil

150g salad leaves, to serve

for the salsa

½ ripe mango, peeled, destoned and finely diced

1 small red chilli, finely diced

4 plum tomatoes, deseeded and finely diced

½ red onion, finely chopped

3 spring onions, finely sliced

2 garlic cloves, finely chopped

a handful of fresh coriander, chopped

juice of 1 lemon or lime

150g salad leaves

sea salt and freshly ground black pepper

1. First make the salsa: Place all the ingredients in a large bowl, mix to combine thoroughly and season to taste.

2. Lightly season the swordfish on both sides. Heat the oil in a griddle pan until really hot and cook the steaks for 2 minutes on each side, then cover, take off the heat and keep in the hot pan for 3–4 minutes.

3. Arrange the salsa on a plate, top with the fish and serve with a side salad of mixed leaves.

TIP Cooking swordfish is easy. The trick is to ensure the griddle pan is nice and hot before you start and to cook it all the way through to the point where the texture is a little flaky but not mushy.

SESAME TUNA STEAK
WITH WOK-FRIED VEGETABLES

Sesame with tuna is one of those classic flavour combinations that I turn to again and again. I love sesame oil too but it has such a strong, distinctive flavour that a little goes a long way.

453 CALORIES | 23G FAT | 4G SATURATES | 4.5G CARBS | 4G SUGAR | 0.5G SALT | 53G PROTEIN | 6G FIBRE

SERVES 4

6 tablespoons sesame seeds

4 x 180g tuna steaks

2 tablespoons olive oil

½ large white onion, thinly sliced

8 asparagus, trimmed and sliced into 5cm pieces

200g fresh spinach

juice of ½ lemon

1 small red bird's eye chilli, very finely chopped (retain the seeds for extra heat)

1 tablespoon sesame oil

sea salt and freshly ground black pepper

4 spring onions, finely sliced

a handful of fresh coriander

1. Spread the sesame seeds out over a large plate and then, one at a time, press the tuna steaks down firmly onto the plate so the seeds stick on all sides.

2. Heat 1 tablespoon oil in a large non-stick frying pan and, when hot, sear the tuna steaks for 1–2 minutes on each side. Take the tuna out of the pan and set aside.

3. Heat the remaining oil in a large wok and cook the onions for 2 minutes, then add the asparagus and stir-fry for a further few minutes.

4. Now add the spinach and stir until it wilts, then add the lemon juice and take off the heat.

5. Add the chilli and sesame oil and mix well, then season to taste.

6. Divide the wok-fried vegetables between four serving plates. Arrange the tuna on top and scatter with spring onion and coriander to garnish.

TIP Nothing is worse than overcooked tuna. It's such a waste of good quality and fairly expensive fish so I always recommend you keep it rare on the inside.

SEA BASS PARCELS

Filling the cavity of a fish with herbs and spices beautifully infuses the flesh with flavour, plus wrapping it in foil keeps it nice and moist.

445 CALORIES | 22G FAT | 5.5G SATURATES | 12G CARBS | 11G SUGAR | 1G SALT | 45G PROTEIN | 8G FIBRE

SERVES 4

- 1 large handful of fresh coriander
- 1 garlic clove, peeled
- 2.5cm cube fresh ginger, grated
- ½ small red bird's eye chilli
- 4 whole sea bass, gutted, cleaned and scaled
- 250ml fish stock
- 50ml light coconut milk
- 4 large carrots, peeled and sliced into matchsticks
- 2 lemons, 1 thinly sliced, 1 quartered
- 600g asparagus, trimmed
- freshly ground black pepper
- squeeze of lemon juice

1. Preheat the oven 180°C/gas mark 4.

2. Place the coriander, garlic, ginger and chilli in a food processor and blend until finely chopped.

3. Rinse out the cavity of each fish under cold running water to ensure it is completely clean and check all the scales have been removed. (You can use the back of a knife to do this, running it in the opposite direction to the scales.)

4. Spread a quarter of the spice mix inside the cavity of each fish and place each one on a piece of lightly oiled foil that has been twisted to form a shallow bowl shape.

5. Mix together the stock and coconut milk and pour over the fish in each foil packet. Add some carrot sticks and a few slices of lemon and cover with another sheet of foil and seal together. Cook in the oven for 20–25 minutes.

6. Meanwhile, place a large griddle pan over a high heat and dry-griddle the asparagus on all sides until nicely charred. Season with a twist of pepper, dress with a squeeze of lemon and keep warm.

7. Check that the fish is cooked through: the flesh should be firm and flake easily, then serve with the grilled asparagus and don't forget to spoon the juices from the parcel over the top.

SEAWEED SALMON

The beauty of this dish is that the seaweed protects the fish while cooking so keeps it beautifully moist. Seaweed is of course a great accompaniment to almost any fish so try this recipe with trout or cod or sea bass or whatever you happen to have to hand.

475 CALORIES | 33G FAT | 6G SATURATES | 0.5G CARBS | 0.5G SUGAR | 0.3G SALT | 42G PROTEIN | 2G FIBRE

SERVES 4

8 nori (seaweed) sheets

1 teaspoon wasabi paste (optional)

4 x 200g skinless salmon fillets

for the marinade

2.5cm cube fresh ginger, grated

juice of ½ lime

a handful of fresh coriander, finely chopped

1 garlic clove, crushed

1 teaspoon sesame oil

1 small red bird's eye chilli, finely chopped

for the pak choi

1 tablespoon olive oil

2 heads pak choi, leaves separated

2 garlic cloves, finely chopped

1. First make the marinade: In a small bowl, mix together the ginger, lime, coriander, garlic, sesame oil and chilli, then set aside.

2. Lay out 4 sheets of seaweed paper on a chopping board. If you are using the wasabi, take a chopstick or knife and run a thin line of paste across each sheet, then lay the salmon on top. Drizzle the marinade over each salmon fillet, then lay a seaweed sheet on top and rest for 2 minutes so the seaweed absorbs the liquid and the flavours. Now fold over all the edges to make a parcel.

3. Place the salmon parcels in a bamboo steamer and steam for 12–15 minutes.

4. Meanwhile, place the oil in a wok over a high heat and stir-fry the pak choi and garlic for a few minutes until wilted.

5. Transfer the salmon to a chopping board and, with a sharp knife, slice each parcel into three or four pieces. Serve with the pak choi on the side.

TIP Wasabi is a Japanese plant in the same family as horseradish, cabbage, and mustard. In its completely natural form, it is a Paleo ingredient and yet sadly, as it's a plant that's hard to grow, the 'wasabi' condiment you're most likely served at sushi restaurants is not wasabi at all. If it is green, it has food colouring in it, and it might also contain some form of starch too. You should be able to find powdered wasabi root at Japanese markets, but be warned that it will be pricey!

ROASTED MONKFISH
WRAPPED IN PROSCIUTTO

Wrapping fish in prosciutto and then roasting it in the oven is such a simple but fail-safe way of achieving really wonderful flavour. Try it with cod and haddock and salmon and chicken. It's always delicious!

573 CALORIES | 29G FAT | 5G SATURATES | 5G CARBS | 4G SUGAR | 3G SALT | 72G PROTEIN | 4G FIBRE

SERVES 4

4 x 350g monkfish tails

60g sun-dried tomatoes in olive oil

12 slices prosciutto or Parma ham

400g rocket leaves

400g asparagus, ends trimmed

1 tablespoon olive oil

for the dressing

4 tablespoons olive oil.

2 tablespoons balsamic vinegar

1 tablespoon Dijon mustard

juice of 1 lemon

1. Preheat the oven to 200°C /gas mark 6.

2. Place the monkfish tails on a chopping board and, using a sharp knife, make a 2.5cm deep incision down the length of the tail.

3. Drain the sun-dried tomatoes on a sheet of kitchen paper to absorb the excess oil, then slice into thin strips and then tuck these slices into the incision you've just made down the length of the fish.

4. Wrap the monkfish with prosciutto so that all the flesh is covered and place on a foil-lined roasting tin. Roast in the oven for 20–25 minutes or until completely cooked through.

5. Meanwhile, whisk all the salad dressing ingredients in a small bowl and then toss over the rocket leaves.

6. Heat a large griddle pan over a medium-high heat and dry-griddle the asparagus spears on all sides until nicely marked. As soon as they're done, dress them with a squeeze of lemon.

7. Serve the fish alongside the asparagus and salad with a few additional sun-dried tomatoes if you like.

SEARED SCALLOPS ON PARSNIP PURÉE

If you reduce the portion size, this makes a great dinner party starter, or even serve on Chinese porcelain spoons as a canapé. As a main course, I recommend you serve this with some wilted spinach on the side.

504 CALORIES | 16G FAT | 3G SATURATES | 26G CARBS | 11G SUGAR | 1G SALT | 56G PROTEIN | 10G FIBRE

SERVES 4

1 whole garlic bulb, sliced in half

4–6 tablespoons olive oil

4–6 large parsnips, peeled and quartered

sea salt and freshly ground black pepper

900g scallops (find the largest you can)

a handful of fresh chives

1. Preheat the oven to 220°C/gas mark 7.

2. Place the garlic bulb halves in a small ovenproof dish and drizzle with olive oil, then wrap in foil and bake in the oven for 30 minutes. Set aside to cool, then squeeze the roasted garlic out of the skin.

3. Bring a pan of water to the boil, reduce to a simmer and cook the parsnips for 18–20 minutes or until soft. Drain, then place in a food processor with the olive oil and roasted garlic flesh. Blend until smooth, then season to taste.

4. Heat a little oil in a large non-stick frying pan over a high heat and sear the scallops on each side until they have browned (about 2 minutes each side, depending on size).

5. Spoon the purée onto each plate. Arrange a few scallops on top and garnish with a scatter of fresh chives.

TIP Eat lots of scallops for a healthy heart. They're full of vitamin B12 (which keeps homocysteine low and therefore protects against heart attacks and strokes) and magnesium (relaxes blood vessels, thus improving blood flow) and potassium (also keeping blood pressure low).

THAI RED CHICKEN CURRY

The Paleo diet is dairy-free but you can use coconut milk for when you're craving something with a lovely creamy texture. However, be aware that coconut milk is high in saturated fat so try and use the 'light' version whenever you can.

324 CALORIES | 8G FAT | 2G SATURATES | 5G CARBS | 3.5G SUGAR | 1G SALT | 56G PROTEIN | 3G FIBRE

SERVES 4

1 tablespoon olive oil

1 large onion, finely chopped

4 skinless chicken breasts (900g), sliced

2.5cm cube fresh ginger, grated

1 garlic clove, crushed

2 tablespoons Thai red curry paste

100ml vegetable stock

50ml light coconut milk

2 chillis, finely chopped

200g fresh spinach

a handful of fresh coriander, chopped

1. Heat the olive oil in a large, non-stick saucepan and sweat the onion for 3–5 minutes, turning constantly.

2. Add the chicken to the pan and cook, stirring, for a further 5 minutes.

3. Add the ginger, garlic, curry paste and stock and cook, stirring, for a minute, then add the coconut milk, reduce the heat to low and simmer, covered, for 12–15 minutes.

4. Remove the lid, add the chilli and spinach and cook for a further 5 minutes, then take off the heat.

5. Divide the curry between four bowls and serve with a scattering of fresh coriander.

TIP As always when buying curry pastes, read the label and check there aren't any preservatives or artificial colours or added flavourings. Brands like Aroy-D and Mae Ploy are Paleo-friendly, or you could always make your own.

CHINESE CHICKEN STIR-FRY

Over the years, I've been very lucky to spend a lot of time in Hong Kong and Shanghai, where I've tasted some of the best Chinese cuisine, with no starch or MSG in sight! In fact, Chinese food, when cooked properly, is very often light and extremely healthy and this stir-fry makes the quickest, easiest, most satisfying weeknight supper.

317 CALORIES | 8G FAT | 1.5G SATURATES | 10G CARBS | 8G SUGAR | 0.4G SALT | 50G PROTEIN | 1.6G FIBRE

SERVES 4

1 tablespoon olive oil

4 large skinless chicken breasts, sliced

1 small red onion, sliced

6–8 button mushrooms, chopped

1 x 225g tin water chestnuts, drained

4 pak choi, leaves separated

1 small red bird's eye chilli, finely chopped

1 teaspoon cracked black pepper

1 tablespoon raw unrefined honey

1 tablespoon sesame oil

a handful of fresh chives, finely chopped

1. Heat ½ tablespoon olive oil in a large non-stick wok over a high heat and stir-fry the chicken until sealed on all sides, then take out of the pan and set aside.

2. Heat the remaining olive oil in the wok, add the onion and mushrooms and stir-fry for 3–4 minutes, then add the water chestnuts, pak choi, chilli and pepper and return the chicken to the pan. Stir-fry over a high heat for 2–3 minutes, stirring all the time.

3. Take the wok off the heat, add the honey and sesame oil and stir to coat all the ingredients.

4. Serve immediately with a scattering of chopped fresh chives.

TIP Most processed honey today has been heated and filtered which sadly robs it of all its many nutritional benefits and therefore, raw honey is a far superior product. It is generally more solid than regular honey, but if you heat it a little it will melt and can then be drizzled.

FISH STEW
WITH BLACK OLIVES

This dish is incredibly simple to make, but tastes delicious and fills you up with high-quality protein so keeps the hunger pangs at bay. It's both a great dinner party recipe and a brilliant weeknight supper option and the leftovers, steeped in the flavours for longer, are even tastier the following day. Serve with some purple-sprouting broccoli or asparagus if you'd like a few greens on the side.

319 CALORIES | 10G FAT | 1.5G SATURATES | 6G CARBS | 5.5G SUGAR | 2G SALT | 50G PROTEIN | 2.6G FIBRE

SERVES 4

1 tablespoon olive oil

1 medium white onion, finely chopped

1 x 400g can chopped tomatoes

2 garlic cloves, finely chopped

250ml vegetable stock

1 teaspoon fennel seeds

1 x 170g can drained pitted black olives

800g skinless white fish, cut into large chunks

300g raw peeled king prawns

a handful of flat-leaf parsley, finely chopped

1. Heat the oil in a large cast iron casserole dish over a high heat and sauté the onions for 2–3 minutes.

2. Add the tomatoes and garlic and cook down for a few minutes, then add the stock, fennel seeds, olives, fish and prawns and reduce the heat to low. Cover and cook for 5 minutes until just opaque (so the fish doesn't fall apart).

3. Remove the lid, turn up the heat and cook for a further 2–3 minutes.

4. Serve immediately with a scattering of fresh parsley.

TIP If you like a varied mix of seafood, you could add some clams and mussels and make it to be more like a bouillabaisse (a traditional French seafood soup).

LEMON THYME CHICKEN

This is wonderful over any kind of wilted greens as they absorb all the lovely cooking juices.

555 CALORIES | 19G FAT | 4G SATURATES | 7G CARBS | 7G SUGAR | 2G SALT | 87G PROTEIN | 3G FIBRE

SERVES 4

1 tablespoon olive oil

sea salt and freshly ground black pepper

1 chicken (approx 2.25kg), cut into 8 pieces

2 lemons, halved

2 tablespoons maple syrup

3 garlic cloves, crushed

170g green olives, pitted

2 sprigs of thyme

180ml vegetable stock

200g spinach

1. Add a drizzle of olive oil to a large cast iron casserole dish and place over a high heat. When the oil is hot, lightly season the chicken pieces with salt and pepper and then sear for about 4 minutes on each side.

2. Squeeze the juice from 2 of the lemon halves over the chicken and add the squeezed skins to the pan. Add the remaining two lemon halves to the pan together with the maple syrup, garlic, olives, thyme and stock.

3. Bring to the boil then lower the heat, cover and simmer for 30 minutes.

4. Serve hot on a bed of spinach or greens of your choice.

TIP Chicken skin has acquired a very bad 'high fat' reputation over the years, which is a shame as it turns out that most of the fat is actually healthy, unsaturated fat, and cooking with the skin keeps the chicken flavourful and moist, which reduces the need for extra seasoning.

TANDOORI CHICKEN

This makes a great alternative roast as it's packed full of flavour and is wonderfully simple to prepare.

754 CALORIES | 15G FAT | 5G SATURATES | 1G CARBS | 0.2G SUGAR | 1G SALT | 153G PROTEIN | 0.9G FIBRE

SERVES 4

1 large (1.75kg) chicken

1 lemon, quartered

sea salt and freshly ground black pepper

90ml light coconut milk

1½ teaspoons ground cumin

1½ teaspoons chilli powder

1 teaspoon ground turmeric

1 teaspoon ground coriander

1 teaspoon garam masala

4 garlic cloves, crushed

for the salad

200g rocket

a handful of fresh coriander

a handful of fresh mint

1. Preheat the oven to 200°C/gas mark 6.

2. Place the chicken in a roasting tin and place the lemon quarters inside the bird. Season lightly with salt and pepper.

3. Place all the remaining ingredients in a bowl and mix together well. Divide this spice mix in half and set one half aside.

4. Baste the chicken thoroughly all over with half the marinade and roast in the oven for 45 minutes, then remove the bird from the oven and baste all over again with the remaining marinade, and then roast for a further 45 minutes or until the thigh juices run clear when tested with a skewer.

5. Serve the chicken with a fresh green herb salad of rocket, coriander and mint.

CHICKEN MINCE BOLOGNESE

This is a lovely twist on an old classic. The chicken mince is a delicious alternative to the traditional beef and, although it's not so common to see in the supermarket, you can buy it very easily at your local butchers, and this way it also comes freshly minced. Plus the sun-dried tomatoes give the dish a wonderfully rich and satisfying flavour, which is of course why we all loved Spag Bol in the first place.

490 CALORIES | 13G FAT | 2.5G SATURATES | 11.5G CARBS | 11G SUGAR | 0.7G SALT | 79G PROTEIN | 4G FIBRE

SERVES 4

for the bolognese

1 tablespoon olive oil

1 small white onion, finely chopped

1¼kg lean chicken mince (ask your butcher)

2 garlic cloves

1 x 400g can chopped tomatoes

1 tablespoon tomato purée

2 tablespoons chopped sun-dried tomatoes

6 plum tomatoes, chopped

sea salt and freshly ground black pepper

a handful of fresh basil, finely chopped

for the courgetti

1 tablespoon olive oil

2 courgettes, peeled into long ribbons

1. First make the bolognese: Place the olive oil in a large cast-iron pan or non-stick saucepan over a high heat and fry the onions, stirring, for 2–3 minutes.

2. Add the chicken mince and cook for 2–3 minutes, then add the garlic, tinned tomatoes, tomato purée, sun-dried tomatoes and plum tomatoes. Season with salt and pepper, stir to combine, then reduce the heat, cover and simmer over a low heat for 15 minutes.

3. Scatter a tablespoon of chopped basil over the pan and stir in well, then cook, uncovered, for a final few minutes.

4. Meanwhile, make the courgetti: In a separate pan, heat the olive oil over a medium heat and toss the courgette ribbons for 2–3 minutes.

5. Divide the courgette pasta between four serving plates. Add a spoon or two of bolognese, garnish with the remaining basil and serve straight away.

TIP Courgette 'pasta' is a genius idea and so versatile. In order to make good long spaghetti-like ribbons, it is worth investing in a spiraliser. However, I have also achieved very good results with a simple and more budget-friendly julienne peeler.

TURKEY MEATBALLS

These meatballs are delicious served with a simple salad, or they go very well with a courgette pasta (see previous page).

394 CALORIES | 19G FAT | 2G SATURATES | 10G CARBS | 6G SUGAR | 1.2G SALT | 43G PROTEIN | 5G FIBRE

SERVES 4

200g mixed salad leaves,
   to serve

for the meatballs

450g turkey mince

1 egg

1 onion, grated

2–3 tablespoons homemade
   or Frank's Hot Wings Sauce
   (see page 75)

1 teaspoon dried Italian
   seasoning

1 teaspoon dried parsley

1 teaspoon garlic powder

1 teaspoon onion powder

½ teaspoon sea salt

½ teaspoon black pepper

60g almond flour

for the topping

60g almond flour

1 teaspoon dried parsley

1 teaspoon crushed black
   peppercorns

1. Preheat the oven to 200°C/gas mark 7 and line a baking tray with foil or parchment paper (for easy clean-up). If using foil, spray with a little coconut oil to prevent sticking.

2. Place all the meatball ingredients in a large bowl and use your hands to mix everything together. Divide the mixture into approximately 20 round balls, then roll them in the topping ingredients to coat lightly and place them on the baking tray.

3. Bake in the oven for 20–25 minutes until browned and cooked all the way through.

4. Serve with a simple green salad.

TIP If you prefer a crisp, brown outer crust, fry the meatballs in a sauté pan in 1 tablespoon coconut oil and cook until browned on all sides, then transfer the pan to the oven (or transfer the meatballs to a baking sheet) and bake until firm.

Grating the onion adds moisture to the meatballs. Grate the onion over the bowl in which you are going to mix the meatballs so none of the liquid is lost.

KLEFTIKO

The verb 'klevo' in Greek means 'to steal' and it's said that when the Greeks were hiding out in the mountains and fighting to liberate themselves from Ottoman rule, they would make this dish in a clay pot and bury it with hot coals under ground until it was done. This way, the cooking smells didn't escape and lead the Ottomans to their hiding places. However, if you don't want to use a clay pot or cook this dish out in your garden, create a parcel for the lamb with parchment paper and foil and this will seal in the heat and cooking juices beautifully.

603 CALORIES | 33G FAT | 13G SATURATES | 0.5G CARBS | 0.5G SUGAR | 0.7G SALT | 76G PROTEIN | 0.6G FIBRE

SERVES 4

2kg leg of lamb on the bone

4 garlic cloves, thinly sliced

sea salt and freshly ground black pepper

1 tablespoon olive oil

juice of 1 lemon

2 tablespoons finely chopped fresh rosemary sprigs

1 whole garlic bulb drizzled in olive oil and wrapped in foil

150g mixed salad leaves

a handful of fresh mint

1. Preheat the oven to 220°C/gas mark 7.

2. Using a sharp knife, make small incisions all over the leg of lamb and slide garlic slivers into each cut. Season the joint all over with salt and pepper and place in a large roasting pan.

3. Place the oil, lemon juice and rosemary in a small bowl and stir well together, then rub this marinade all over the lamb joint. Leave for at least 20 minutes for the flavours to infuse.

4. Create a tent for the lamb to cook in by enclosing the pan in a large sheet of baking parchment, covered with a large sheet of foil. Cook in the oven for 20 minutes.

5. Uncover the meat, reduce the heat to 180°C/gas mark 4 and cook the lamb for 1 hour, then turn the oven off and leave the meat in the hot oven for a final 30 minutes.

6. Serve the lamb with its cooking juices, together with a salad of mixed leaves and fresh mint.

TIP There is nothing like this dish. It's easy to prepare and although it does take a while to cook, this is the reason why it falls off the bone and melts in the mouth.

LAMB SKEWERS

Lamb is a very sturdy meat so you can add heavy flavours to it without overpowering it, unlike fish or white meat. The maple syrup and soy sauce in this recipe go fantastically well with lamb, so make sure the meat is thoroughly coated with the marinade.

446 CALORIES | 23G FAT | 9G SATURATES | 8.5G CARBS | 6G SUGAR | 1.8G SALT | 48G PROTEIN | 3.5G FIBRE

SERVES 4

- 2 garlic cloves, crushed
- 2 tablespoons coconut aminos
- 2 teaspoons tomato purée
- 1 tablespoon maple syrup
- a few sprigs of fresh thyme, leaves picked
- 900g lean boneless lamb, cut into 2.5cm cubes
- 1 medium white onion, quartered
- 1 red pepper, deseeded and cut into 2.5cm cubes
- 12 button mushrooms
- 150g olives
- 150g rocket leaves, to serve

1. Preheat the oven to 180°C/gas mark 4.

2. Place the garlic, coconut aminos, tomato purée, maple syrup and thyme in a large bowl and mix together well. Add the lamb and toss in the marinade until thoroughly coated, then cover and place in the refrigerator for 20 minutes.

3. Load each skewer with alternating cubes of lamb, onion, pepper and mushroom and then place on a foil-lined tray.

4. Place the skewers in the oven and cook for 16 minutes for rare or 20 minutes for medium–well-done. Alternatively, grill under a high heat, turning and browning all sides until cooked through but still a little pink in the middle.

5. Allow to rest for a minute or two, then serve with a small bowl of olives and a side of fresh rocket leaves.

GRILLED LAMB CHOPS ON CARROT PURÉE
WITH ROASTED GARLIC

This is a great midweek supper that only uses a handful of ingredients and is very simple to prepare, yet deliciously satisfying. The carrot purée can be used as a side in many other dishes, such as the Lemon Thyme Chicken on page 129.

486 CALORIES | 26G FAT | 10G SATURATES | 9G CARBS | 8G SUGAR | 0.6G SALT | 51G PROTEIN | 5G FIBRE

SERVES 4

600g carrots, peeled and roughly chopped

12 lamb chops or cutlets (about 110g each), trimmed of fat

2 garlic cloves, thinly sliced

4 sprigs fresh rosemary, cut into thirds

2 tablespoons olive oil

sea salt and freshly ground black pepper

1. Preheat the oven 180°C/gas mark 4.

2. Place the carrots in a saucepan of boiling water and cook for 20–25 minutes until soft.

3. Meanwhile, using a sharp knife, cut a few incisions in the lamb and slide in a few garlic slivers and a sprig of rosemary in each chop. Place on a foil-lined baking tray and roast in the oven for 10–12 minutes (depending on size).

4. Drain the carrots, transfer to a food processor and add the olive oil. Season with salt and pepper to taste and whiz to a purée.

5. Serve the lamb with the carrot purée and garnish with some fresh rosemary.

TIP The beta-carotene that carrots are incredibly rich in can slow down signs of ageing as it acts as an antioxidant and protects against cell damage. It's then converted to vitamin A in the liver and there also assists with flushing toxins out of the body.

BEEF BURGER
IN AN AUBERGINE BUN

You do need a knife and fork to eat this but it has a really nice texture and is a much better alternative to eating the burger on its own.

373 CALORIES | 25G FAT | 9G SATURATES | 7.5G CARBS | 6G SUGAR | 1.7G SALT | 26G PROTEIN | 5G FIBRE

SERVES 4

1 aubergine, sliced into
    8 rounds

olive oil, for frying

red onion, thinly sliced

1 little gem lettuce

1 tablespoon homemade
    ketchup (see page 26)

for the burgers

450g lean beef mince

1 egg

1 tablespoon Dijon mustard

½ red onion, finely chopped

1 garlic clove, crushed

1 teaspoon salt

½ teaspoon pepper

1 teaspoon onion powder
    (optional)

½ teaspoon cayenne pepper

1 tablespoon chopped
    fresh parsley

for the guacamole

1 avocado

juice of 1 lime

a handful of coriander

1 red or green chilli, deseeded

1. Place all the burger ingredients in a large bowl and mix together with your hands, then shape into four burgers.

2. Spray a non-stick frying pan with a little olive oil and fry the burgers over a medium heat for 3–4 minutes on each side or until cooked to your liking. (Alternatively, oven cook them for 20–25 minutes in a 200°C/gas mark 6 oven, but don't forget to flip them halfway through.)

3. Meanwhile, heat a little oil in a second non-stick pan and fry the aubergine slices over a medium to high heat for 2–3 minutes on each side.

4. Place all the guacamole ingredients in a bowl and mash everything together with a fork.

5. Stack the burgers on an aubergine slice and layer up with salad, red onion, guacamole and tomato ketchup and serve immediately.

TIP When cooking burgers, try to resist flipping too often. It is tempting but they can fall apart if you do.

SIRLOIN STEAK

Sirloin is a lovely cut of meat as it has just the right amount of fat to keep it lovely and tender while it cooks, and this is simply the best way to cook it. I recommend you use a barbecue with a lid or a large, smoking-hot griddle pan.

927 CALORIES | 36G FAT | 14G SATURATES | 2G CARBS | 2G SUGAR | 1G SALT | 148G PROTEIN | 0.8G FIBRE

- -

SERVES 4–6

2–3kg sirloin steak

2 teaspoons olive oil

sea salt and freshly ground
  black pepper

tinned hearts of palm, sliced

200g green salad, including
  rocket

balsamic vinaigrette
  (see page 98)

1. Preheat the grill to at least 220°C/gas mark 8.

2. Rub the steak all over with a little oil and season with salt and pepper.

3. Sear the steak on the grill for 2–3 minutes, then turn and sear again for another 2–3 minutes. Repeat this until the beef has rotated fully and is seared on all sides, then rest for 15 minutes. (If you are using a barbecue with a lid, ensure it is closed while the meat rests.)

4. Transfer the meat to a board and rest for a few further minutes, then slice into large steaks.

5. Serve with sliced hearts of palm and some fresh green salad, drizzled with a little balsamic vinaigrette.

FILLET STEAK
WITH CARAMELISED ONIONS

A good fillet steak should be so tender you can cut it with a fork. It's often a very expensive choice on a restaurant menu and so it's much better to make it at home. I recommend you source it from your local butcher and don't overcook it, and also don't forget to take the steaks out of the fridge 1–2 hours prior to cooking, to bring them up to room temperature. This helps the meat brown nicely as you don't waste heat from the pan taking the chill off its surface area.

760 CALORIES | 46G FAT | 10G SATURATES | 18G CARBS | 15G SUGAR | 0.3G SALT | 46G PROTEIN | 7G FIBRE

SERVES 2

2 x 200g fillet steaks

3 tablespoons extra virgin olive oil

sea salt and freshly ground black pepper

225g fresh mushrooms (any variety), chopped

1 tablespoon chopped fresh thyme

180ml red wine

160g carrots

for the caramelised onions

3 onions, thinly sliced

2 tablespoons extra virgin olive oil, plus more as needed

sea salt and freshly ground black pepper, to taste

1. First make the caramelised onions: Place the onions in a large frying pan over a medium-high heat, cover and cook, stirring infrequently, until they are dry and almost sticking to the pan (about 20 minutes).

2. Stir in the oil and a large pinch of salt, then reduce the heat to medium-low and cook, stirring occasionally and adding oil as needed to keep them from sticking without getting greasy, for 40–60 minutes, depending on how you want them. Season to taste and set aside.

3. Meanwhile, brush the steaks all over with a little olive oil and season lightly with salt and pepper. Place a large griddle pan over a medium high heat and, when hot, add the steaks and cook for 2–3 minutes on each side (or until done to your liking), then remove from the pan and set aside.

4. Add the remaining olive oil to the pan, add the mushrooms and cook over a high heat for 5–10 minutes until golden brown.

5. Add the wine and thyme to the pan, bring to a simmer and cook for 3–4 minutes until the wine has reduced slightly.

6. Plate the steaks with a spoonful of sauce, the caramelised onions on the side and a few carrots too, if you like.

DESSERTS

APPLE PIE

I try to avoid desserts as a rule, but of course there are always those days when one savoury course just isn't enough and what you really want is something sweet. This apple pie is still Paleo and will hopefully hit the spot.

442 CALORIES | 21G FAT | 1.7G SATURATES | 49G CARBS | 42G SUGAR | 0.1G SALT | 12G PROTEIN | 6G FIBRE

SERVES 4

5 Granny Smith apples, peeled, cored and sliced

½ teaspoon cinnamon

juice of 2 oranges

3 tablespoons maple syrup

for the topping

3 tablespoons maple syrup

150g almond flour or coconut flour

3 egg whites, whisked

1. Preheat the oven to 180°C/gas mark 4.

2. Place the apples, cinnamon, orange juice and maple syrup in a large bowl and mix together until the apple pieces are thoroughly coated. Tip the fruit into a baking tin and bake for 35 minutes.

3. Meanwhile, place all the topping ingredients in a bowl and mix together thoroughly.

4. When the apple is cooked, spread the topping mix evenly over the top, then return to the oven and bake for a further 30 minutes. Serve slightly warm.

TIP   Any leftovers will also make a very tasty breakfast.

BANANA SOUFFLÉ

The more you whisk the eggs, the higher the soufflés rise in the oven...

189 CALORIES | 8G FAT | 2.5G SATURATES | 16G CARBS | 14G SUGAR | 0.4G SALT | 12G PROTEIN | 0.7G FIBRE

SERVES 4-6

2 ripe bananas

1 teaspoon vanilla paste
  (or extract)

2 tablespoons maple syrup
  (at room temp)

6 eggs

1. Preheat the oven to 200°C/gas mark 6.

2. Mash the bananas with the vanilla in a bowl, then add the maple syrup and mix in well.

3. Separate the eggs and, using an electric mixer, whisk the egg whites until they form soft peaks. Add the yolks to the banana mix and stir well. Gently fold in the 2 mixtures together and divide between 4–6 silicone ramekin dishes (if not using silicone, oil very lightly).

4. Bake in the oven for 15 minutes until well risen. Serve immediately.

TIP Make sure you whisk your eggs in a very clean mixing bowl. I always rinse with boiling water and dry with a clean tea towel to ensure it's completely free from grease.

COCONUT EGG CUSTARD

This is a very light dessert. The custard should have a lovely silky smooth texture and the trick to achieving this is to cook it for a long time over a very low heat.

234 CALORIES | 15G FAT | 6G SATURATES | 9G CARBS | 7.5G SUGAR | 0.5G SALT | 16G PROTEIN | 0.8G FIBRE

SERVES 4

8 eggs
200ml light coconut milk
1 teaspoon ground cinnamon
2 tablespoons maple syrup
4 kumquats

1. Crack the eggs into a large bowl and whisk together. Add the coconut milk, cinnamon and maple syrup and whisk to combine, then divide between four ramekin dishes.

2. Bring a saucepan of water to the boil, and place the ramekins in a steamer on top of the pan. Turn the heat down as low as you can and simmer for 18-20 minutes.

3. Serve with fresh kumquats or fruit of your choice.

TIP Cinnamon is loaded with antioxidants, more than any other spice (even super-spices like garlic and oregano), plus it helps the body fight infections and repairs tissue damage.

BANANA FRITTERS

This is the perfect, easy dish to rustle up in minutes when you really need something for that sweet tooth.

658 CALORIES | 39G FAT | 17G SATURATES | 47G CARBS | 21G SUGAR | 0.3G SALT | 19G PROTEIN | 15G FIBRE

SERVES 4

4 ripe bananas

2 eggs

150g almond flour

coconut oil, for frying

150g coconut flour

1. Place the banana in a large bowl and, with a fork, mash until it forms a thick paste. Add the eggs and almond flour and whisk until combined.

2. Heat a little coconut oil in a large non-stick frying pan over a medium heat. When hot, drop small spoonfuls of banana batter into the oil and press down flat.

3. Sprinkle with a little coconut flour and fry for a few minutes, then flip the fritter over with a spatula and cook on the other side. Repeat until all the batter is used up. Serve warm.

TIP Bananas are very interesting in relation to their carbohydrate and sugar content. They are very sweet, especially when ripe and they do contain 14-15 grams of sugar, yet they have a low-GI value, which means the sugar doesn't result in a short, fast energy spike. This is largely down to their high fibre content as this helps regulate digestion (i.e. the conversion of carbs to simple sugars), and in particular to a type of fibre called pectin, as this moderates the impact of banana consumption on our blood sugar and supports our overall digestive health.

COCONUT BERRIES

This is a delicious, light dessert – perfect for summer when so many berries are in season. Obviously the coconut milk does have a high fat content, so use sparingly if you are trying to keep the weight off or save this up for the weekend. You could also try this with light coconut milk, but you don't get quite as much of the thick creamy part as you need so it's not as tasty.

141 CALORIES | 9G FAT | 8G SATURATES | 11G CARBS | 10G SUGAR | 0G SALT | 2G PROTEIN | 3G FIBRE

- -

SERVES 4

coconut cream from 1 x 400g
    tin coconut milk (reserve
    the milk for a smoothie,
    see pages 39–43)
1 tablespoon raw honey
    (at room temperature)
1 teaspoon vanilla extract
450g mixed berries
mint, for garnish

1. Open the tin of coconut milk and separate the thick creamy part, reserving the thinner milk for use in a smoothie. Keeping the tin in the fridge for a few hours will help that process.

2. Place the coconut cream in a bowl and, using an electric whisk, fluff it up into soft peaks. Add the honey and vanilla and whisk a little more.

3. Scatter a few berries into the bottom of each glass and top with a layer of coconut cream, then repeat both these steps until you reach the top. Garnish with a sprig of mint and serve immediately.

- -

TIP Because of their fibre and liquid content, berries give you a nice sense of fullness, which means they round off a meal very nicely. They're also chock-full of antioxidants too.

INDEX

THANK YOU

I would like to thank everyone at Kyle Books who have given me the opportunity to showcase a long-held passion of mine. This is the first opportunity I have had to write a diet plan and I know it works as I live this plan every day. A big thank you to Kyle and Vicki for all the fine details being ironed out so well.

To my wife Jane and my daughters Eleanor and GG. I never tire of cooking for you.

A big thank you also to my manager Kathy Carter who has been a brilliant friend and offered fantastic guidance.

And big thanks also to Pat Carlson and Brandon Eilers for helping me in the kitchen.